You're Not My Dream Date Either!

By Carl Birkmeyer

Copyright 2011 – Carl Birkmeyer

For Leonard and Laura, who believed.

Table of Contents

Introduction

When we're in our early teens and just starting to feel that incredible surge of hormones, we develop all kinds of dreams and hopes for the future. For men, most of our dreams at that age involve careers – astronaut, sports star, president, etc. My life plan was to play center field for the Baltimore Orioles during the day and fight crime at night, returning home to the adoring arms of my wife, Valerie Bertinelli. For women, most of their teen dreams involved their future mate, their wedding, and their life together. They also had career and life goals, but the goal foremost in their minds was their lasting relationship and marriage. Most women use fairy tales, movies, and other forms of fiction to develop a picture of their dream date at that time and they have a strong vision of what their mate and their life should be. At the same time, men are concentrating on sex, not long relationships, and they use the Sports Illustrated swimsuit edition to develop a picture of their dream date.

As we get older, those dreams from our early teens tend to fade away, especially those involving careers. We realize that we're not good enough at math to work for NASA, our guitar playing reminds people of Billy Mays more than Brian May, or we find ourselves working in a different career because that's where our first job took us. As our work life continues, we adjust our dream career and life based on how it all unfolds. Though I tried for quite a while, it became apparent that I wasn't going to move from being a video guy to being a highly successful crime fighter, and not just because my house didn't have a cave underneath it for costume storage. The reality of life and our abilities takes hold and we adjust our plans accordingly.

That's NOT a bad thing. You have to live life on reality's terms. Though I wasn't able to become a center fielder for the Orioles, I was able to use my skills at videography to work for the team's video production department. I realized that my skills were in video production, not crime fighting or hitting a baseball, and I adjusted my career goals to fit that and now I run a small video production department for the government during the day and direct baseball games at night. I took my early childhood dreams and fit them around my skills and abilities to create a damn good life for myself.

However, a great many women, especially those who didn't marry their high school sweetheart, don't change or adjust that dream image of their mate. Ever. Their life experience, their reality, none of it has any impact on that idealized and unrealistic image of their dream date. They may allow for a little graying of the hair but that's the only deviation from the dream that is accepted. The problem is that unchanging image is of someone who just doesn't exist. Both sides of the dating picture are then forced to deal with that idealized image and the frustration women feel at not finding it available out there to date.

That's compounded by the completely changed landscape of dating when you're over thirty-five versus when you're in your twenties. When you're dating at 21, there is a virtually unlimited field of potential dates. The only people not on the market are those sickeningly-sweet couples who are "high school sweethearts," and they'll be divorced and joining us in the dating pool soon enough.

Picture a store where instead of clothes you're buying a date. In your twenties, you're shopping in a five-story building with lots of departments that are fully stocked. Looking for an athletic blonde who likes Alice Cooper? There are ten of them on the second floor. Brunettes who like to go camping? Check out Aisle Seven. You can move from section to section until you find an area that suits your needs and there are hundreds of sections. It's fun to shop around in the areas you like and it's a little easier to find something that fits. When you're in the Athletic Blonde Section, there are dozens, with all kinds of taste in music to pick from. The product is also fairly new to the store so it's fresh, bright, and generally happy.

As soon as you hit 35 or so, the dating store changes from Saks Fifth Avenue to a food store in Ethiopia. When you get to the section you like, it's suddenly empty and so are the two sections nearby. There's not even an Athletic Blonde Section, let alone the chance to find one with similar musical tastes to yours. You end up searching the store for hours until you finally find the basement and discover the only department that's packed; The Scratch and Dent Section. You know, the section that has slightly damaged floor models, returns, and items that just simply refused to sell no matter how many times they went on sale. Even when you manage to spot something from your favorite section that's moved to the Scratch and Dent Section, it's totally different when you get close to it. That athletic blonde who likes Alice Cooper also has seven cats, two dogs, four goats, and believes soap and shampoo are tools of Satan.

Don't get me wrong. Not all of the pieces in the scratch and dent section are unusable. Heck, a lot of them seem very nice. However, there's a reason that they're in the scratch and dent section. The scratches and dents of furniture translate into unrealistic expectations, lack of self-knowledge, emotional problems, and just plain wear and tear in the human beings. Not all of the merchandise is bad, but all of it needs a little bit of work in order to make it a usable item. The main difference between furniture and people in the Scratch and Dent Section is that furniture knows why it's in the scratch and dent section and most people don't. They expect their potential mates to be the same dream date they fantasized about at the age of 14 and completely ignore the fact that they themselves are not the fantasy ideal that they're demanding from others. They're looking for something that doesn't exist and they blame everything but their vision for the fact that they can't see their imaginary ideal in their dates.

That's the fundamental message of this book – **the reason that you do not have a solid relationship is you.** There is no other reason. Not bad luck, not because you "attract jerks," and not because there aren't any good men or women out there. It's you. You're the only thing that never changes in your dating life.

The problem comes from the thousands of books, friends, movies, TV shows, and magazines that insist on telling people, especially women, that it's everybody's fault but theirs. Or, they'll try to convince them to change something superficial in order to find a partner, when the real issues are much deeper. Our married friends aren't much help either, as they insist that we just "need to find the right person." Most of us lack the self-awareness to know when that person even shows up.

I remember a friend giving me a book on dating that stated that there were three different types of people, visually oriented, audio oriented, and print oriented. In order to get the woman I wanted, I was supposed to find out what orientation she was and then use the proper words for that type. That's right, if she was an auditory person, I was supposed to use phrases like, "that rings a bell" and "sounds good to me." I don't know what's sadder, that someone actually published that book or that I actually tried it. That's how desperate I was to find a simple solution to my dating difficulties. What I needed to do was look inside myself, at the choices I was making, and then examine why those choices were not making me happy. It's not easy. It's very hard to do, but being hard is what makes it so great when it finally works out.

I blame the lottery. Most of us look at dating as we do the lottery. We buy ticket after ticket, hoping that one of them will be a winner and we'll suddenly become rich and famous. There's no work involved, all you have to do is keep buying tickets and eventually something good will come of it, most likely happiness. That's a terribly destructive way of thinking, but we use that theory in dating all of the time. Just keep doing the same thing you've been doing, dating the same way and the same type of people, and eventually you'll find the right person for you. Just as 99.9 percent of lottery ticket-buyers are disappointed, so, too, will you be when you approach dating that way. The people who find riches don't buy lottery tickets; they work hard and change things when they don't work. In order to succeed in dating, you have to work hard and change the things that don't work, even if that thing you have to change is you.

What I'm trying to do with this book is help you see how you've become set in your dating habits without even knowing it. That your lack of success is not solely due to the condition of the dating pool, but more due to your preconceptions and beliefs about dating.

This book contains twenty guidelines for dating that will point out flaws and misconceptions people our age have about dating. The majority of the guidelines are for women because women read books and men don't. Both sexes can learn from reading all of the guidelines and seeing how they apply to your life. I guarantee that at least two of the guidelines will apply to your dating life and that if you work hard to accept and apply the guidelines, you'll have a more rewarding dating life.

Why is Dating Doubly Difficult At Our Age?

Or

The Blender Theory

When you're 21 and dating, the world is new to you. You're still learning and growing and developing a life. Life is generally filled with just surviving – your first job, your first disaster, your first place to live. Even if things aren't perfect, there's the excitement of building upon what you have and believing that you will be able to make things better.

At that stage, everything is building up to your core life. You begin to lose the friendships that were based on location and begin to build relationships based on interests and compatibility. You begin to sift through jobs, searching for a career and meaning in your professional life. A lot of hard lessons are learned and remembered, wearing away the rough edges in what will become "you." Elderly relatives pass away and friends start to marry and have children. You start to develop patterns of behavior that aren't based on getting drunk or getting laid. You grow up.

If you have a significant relationship at the time, especially one that involves marriage, you experience all of these things together. The two of you formulate your responses together, creating what is supposed to be an unbreakable bond (all of you divorced people can join me in saying "Hah!"). Your early apartments or houses become joint projects, with both of you intertwined in all decisions. Hobbies develop into interests and then become joint interests. The two of you are like strawberries in a blender, merging into one big goopy mess when you're hit with the blades of life.

The blender ingredients are a lot different once you've passed the age of 35 because your life is pretty much set. Most people have generally found a career, or at least a decent job. You've found a place to live and it's decorated in a style you like, with mementos that are meaningful to you. By now, you've spent years with your hobbies and they've become an integral part of you. If you ski, you have a place that you go and people that you ski with. You have a favorite beach, favorite pizza place, and a favorite style of dress. All of your likes and dislikes are established. You really aren't even looking for new hobbies or interests because you're happy with yours.

Instead of two strawberries going into the blender you've got two large ice cubs. Our lives and our personality are frozen and aren't soft like those young strawberries. When you try and create a smooth mix, there is a lot of rattling around and denting of the cubes and a lot of times the ice refuses to mix and the blender burns out. Sometimes the cubes even fly out of the blender. Even when the two cubes mix, there are always chunks and the mix is nowhere near as smooth as the one made with strawberries.

That hardening of who we have become is not conducive to establishing a relationship. The heart of any good relationship is based on sharing and trusting. Instead of looking for a person to develop life with, we're looking for someone to integrate into our already-formed life. If we ski, we want somebody who skis. We're not interested in learning how to ski together, or even teaching somebody how to ski. Our instinct is to find somebody to come on our ski trips with us, not plan new ski trips together.

You're probably thinking, "Give the skiing example a break," but I bring this up with good reason. It involves a woman I wanted to meet, Christine.

I met Christine online and we had a few brief e-mail conversations. She seemed pleasant and interesting and I thought we might hit it off. She had a few listed hobbies, including skiing, both water and snow, and said that she loved the beach, which is something we both would have in common. Attractive and about my age, I thought we had a couple of other things in common and we had very nice e-mail conversations, so I moved it up to the next stage, a phone call.

Christine called me and we had a pleasant couple of minutes of small talk before she said, "I've got a couple of things I want to ask you." I told her to go ahead, figuring it would be the

13

usual – any kids, pets, or debilitating illnesses? Oh no, I should have been so lucky.

"Okay, do you like the beach?" she began.

"Absolutely," I replied. "I love it, whether it's swimming or sitting …

"Okay, thanks," she interrupted. "What about water skiing?"

"I've never tried it," I replied. "I've always wanted to, but things have just never worked out that I've had the opportunity."

"Uh-huh," she replied, slightly distracted. I could hear a faint sound in the background, but I couldn't quite place it. "Do you snow ski?" she continued.

"No. I tried it once and was completely inept. It seemed like it would have been fun, but I fell down trying to get on the ski lift and it just went downhill from there," I replied, trying to inject a little humor with a bad pun.

"Okay," she said, making that sound again. Suddenly it hit me – the sound was that of a pen on paper and the resulting rustling of the paper. She had a checklist and was going down the list! That was the sound, her marking my answers on the list.

"Do you like to vacation in Ocean City or Rehoboth?" she asked, oblivious to my newfound knowledge. I answered the question, and now could focus on nothing but the sound of her marking my answers down on paper. I felt like Tom Hanks after he cracked the DaVinci Code and I became a little too obsessed with working her checklist. My first instinct was to rebel and start giving fake answers, but I behaved myself and answered all of the questions honestly. I would have even used a number two pencil if I had one at the time.

As the questions ended, it was clear that I had failed to answer the checklist properly, as the conversation became forced. She brought up the skiing questions again; I guess because you're always supposed to double-check your work. I did my part, giving the same answer, although I did phrase it slightly differently.

When I answered "no" again, she immediately began to make excuses to end the conversation. You know, something like

15

"my laundry is finished," or "my hair's on fire" or some other lame excuse that everybody knows is fake. I asked if I could have her number to call her and she told me not to worry, that she'd call me in a day or two, but she just had to go now. As I knew I was clearly done in her mind, I couldn't resist asking, "How many did I get wrong on the checklist?" Her response was to say "How..." and then hang up.

I did have it figured right. She had a checklist and if the man did not match the items on that list, he was through. The checklist didn't involve the important things – character, personality, stability, but instead focused on life activities. If you wanted to date Christine, you had to meet her life on her life's terms. It didn't matter to her if you were honest or if you had had more affairs than Bill Clinton. As long as you could ski, you could get a date with Christine. She had forgotten about one of the joys of a new relationship – learning your partner's interests and sharing them. Her activities were set and she wanted someone whose activities were the exact same as hers because she had no intention of merging her life with anyone.

Granted, Christine is an extreme example, but it does illustrate a common problem for those of us wandering through the dating store. We forget that we need to share our lives. We have to accept another's interests, families and friends.

It's hard, I know. It takes work, work that isn't necessary when you start your life together at 21. We have to fight our natural urges to be brief and our desires to have our new partner accept us as we are. We have to share all of the stories and histories that have made us this way. In addition, we have to share their stories and listen to what makes them who and what they are. It's hard work, but we have to try new things and create new, shared experiences. We have to let the blades of the blender work by melting a little bit more with each turn.

Yes, we have now developed who and what we are. Our core is set. That doesn't mean that we can't learn new things or enjoy new activities and people. A set core of "youness" just means that you must set aside some time to do your core activities, whether it's alone or with your partner. Rather than getting disappointed when your mate doesn't share all of them, relish the fact that when they're doing their core activities that don't interest you, you can do those activities that are important just to you. And go skiing once in a while.

Guideline #1

Learn to Share Again for the First Time

Or

Give up the Clicker

Nobody likes to share. If I order a dessert, I want to finish

off that dessert myself, not end up giving half of it to somebody

I'm dining with. I'm perfectly fine with a dessert swap – giving

half of mine for half of yours, but I'm not a big fan of non-

reciprocal giving (that's a great government term for not sharing,

isn't it?). If I'm that way with chocolate mousse cake, just imagine

how I am with hobbies.

If you've been living alone for a while, and most of the

target audience of this book will have spent a fair amount of time

living on their own, routines and habits have become more and

more ingrained. Our likes and dislikes harden and our world view

starts to narrow. Why try the new Indian restaurant when you love the Italian place down the street? Go to a baseball game when you don't like sports? Attend a musical when you hated seeing *The Wiz* in 1979? Oh yes, it's easy to find arguments for not changing or doing something new or different, but that's precisely why you must do it.

There's not a match alive that has the exact same interests and experiences that you have. So if you want to have a truly great relationship you're going to have to share some of your interests and mix with some of hers. You can't take the attitude of this person who responded to me on an Internet dating service. I asked, "what were some of her interests that she might want to share" and this was her response:

> *As far as interests, I don't have any that I need to share w/anyone; most can't be shared. I enjoy baking, love movies, routinely work out and read when I can. My belief in having interests in a relationship is not necessarily sharing the same but that my partner would respect me and my interests.*

Wow! She had no interest in sharing her interests and merely wanted to be left alone to do her thing. It morphed into a sign of respect too, that a good partner would respect her interests by not wanting to share them with her. So a large portion of her life would permanently be shut off to her partner. That's not the key to a successful relationship. I enjoy almost all the activities she listed and all of them can and should be shared, whether it seems to be a solitary activity or not. I had a great friend who had the same interests as the woman above and we were able to share them a great deal. For example, I love to bake so we would pick out recipes together, buy the ingredients together, make them together, and then enjoy the final result together. All of that didn't have to be done together, but the activity of baking can easily be shared. As can reading. Maybe it's as simple as sitting together on the porch while reading. Or hitting a used bookstore and sharing your finds. Do what you can to share your interests together, both big and small.

I took up SCUBA diving last year and it would be great if I had a partner who loved to SCUBA dive as well. However, they don't have to do that at all. If they like the water then they could come on a SCUBA trip and snorkel while I dive. Or we could journey to a tropical island and I could SCUBA while she did something she enjoyed. There are all kinds of ways to share an interest and a life without actually doing the exact same thing.

Not everything has to be shared either. It is important that everybody has their own thing, whether it's a cheese bread recipe that is their specialty or a certain hobby that they prefer to do by themselves. I would be happy to take up fishing or skiing or other hobbies, but I don't have an interest in say, knitting. However, my partner could knit or sew while I cook or read. I would also be more than happy to have conversations about the colors, patterns, styles, etc. that are involved in knitting. I would still make some attempt to share some of it. Not as much as with other interests, but enough to show that I am interested in what makes my partner happy.

A successful relationship must involve breaking down walls and building new interconnecting pathways. Sometimes those walls are made of paper and sometimes it seems like they're made of solid steel. But they must be knocked down and you must

allow others to walk through them in order to have a truly great

relationship. And don't forget to share your dessert!

Guideline #2

You're In Control of Who You Date

Or

Stop Blaming Me for Your Past

"All men are dogs."

"All the good men are taken."

"Every guy I date cheats on me."

I'm sure that every woman has said some variation of the above lines and every guy has heard them too. A lot of women even combine them into one huge statement – "All the good men are taken, so I end up with the cheaters, that's how I know all men are dogs." Nope, we're not. As a matter of fact, most men are pretty good guys. It's just that you always pick the rotten guys in the group.

The excuse given all the time is that "I need a man that I'm attracted to," but that's a smokescreen to cover poor decision-making. It assumes that an initial and superficial attraction is the main ingredient in a successful relationship. Attraction is not necessarily a good thing. We're attracted to fatty foods, flying by jumping off a cliff, and a host of other activities that aren't always healthy or good for us. We can recognize that eating an entire chocolate cream pie isn't good for us. Why then do we refuse to admit that dating a guy that offers instant attraction also isn't always good for us? Sure, a little pie is great now and then, but it can't be the majority of your diet.

Here's a direct quote from a friend's e-mail lamenting her months of bad dates and what she considers her ideal man:

Maybe I'm asking for too much. You know... I don't want "rich".... I want a good soul, a fun soul, someone who works hard, plays hard and will make me laugh and be my best friend.

That's a pretty nice description of a great date. I think it's what we all really want. She went on to describe one of the two guys she had been dating recently. She had just dumped him.

He was really sweet and we had fun. cute, but not handsome. great smile. Intellectually and interest wise... we had great conversations on all kinds of things and I liked the symphony, opera, museum things we did together.

What was her reason for dumping him? She didn't get that feeling "where I feel like I want to jump out of my skin and right into theirs." That feeling comes about in the movies and in Barry Manilow songs, not in real life. She wasn't focusing on what she had, which was the best friend she described and claimed she desperately wanted. She was focusing on something not real, an imagined perfect person who will never exist. Nobody could meet those expectations. She had a preconceived notion of how she should have felt that prevented her from actually enjoying what she was feeling.

It's important to ignore our preconceived notions and break out of our traditional dating molds and search for new people, new opportunities, and new ideas. Expand that comfort zone. If you can't have a successful relationship with the people you're meeting, try meeting new kinds of people. It's easy to just look for the athletic guy or the suit guy or whatever your particular initial taste happens to be. But it's clearly not working because you haven't found anyone. If it were working, you wouldn't be reading this book and you wouldn't be alone. Take a chance and get to know different people. Date them. Don't concentrate on what they're doing that's different, concentrate on what they're doing right. Enjoy the moment for what it is, not what it should be.

Sure, we'd all like that magic moment in Lifetime movies where everything goes perfectly on the first date. The date where you can't wait to get home and call your best friend and tell them all about this wonderful new person and how they may be "the one." It's how I felt when I first tasted Kate Mantilini's Dark Chocolate Dipped Cheesecake on a Stick. I was positive that I had found the perfect dessert for me. It would never bore me and we seemed to get along so well. It had everything I needed and it was such a pleasure to get to know it. I had to have that dessert again and again. Unfortunately, my stomach ballooned out, I tired of the taste, and it didn't nourish me. It filled a specific need, but it wasn't satisfying to the core. I was reacting to a fantasy that came about instantly and that fantasy just doesn't happen in one night or one weekend. It takes work and a lot of time. It's also important to keep in mind that in those Lifetime movies that begin with such great dates, the guy always turns out to be a murderer.

Guideline #3

Instant Attraction is Not a Good Thing

Or

Don't Eat That Fried Twinkie With Chocolate Sauce!

I think we've all run into the person who believes in love at first sight and other Disney propaganda. Never mind that mutual love and respect can only come after you spend time getting to know each other. These people want Prince Charming to come along and magically sweep them off their feet, just as he did in the movies. In the real world, however, the five-minute Prince Charming always ends up being Prince Shallow. Here are some actual ads from a dating service, completely unedited:

"One look and you'll just know. It's so true isn't it?" (34 and never married)

"I'm a true believer in 'the spark.' I can tell within 5 minutes if I click with someone and that's all I look for. I'm very picky, but only because I don't like to waste anyone's time or my own. If I don't think there is chemistry from the start, I don't proceed." (38 and never married)

"I'm not sure what I'm looking for, to be honest. I know that as soon as I meet him, we'll know we were meant for each other." (43 and never married)

As soon as she meets him, she'll know that they were meant for each other. Think about that for a minute. Think of the pressure she's putting on the first two minutes of that date. Can anyone survive that kind of scrutiny? What can you possibly learn or know about a person in ten minutes? Or one date? You wouldn't pick a car in ten minutes so why would you pick a mate for life in ten minutes? Heck, think of all the times that you stumbled or didn't have a good ten minutes in a conversation. Would you want your future to be judged on that? Yet it happens all the time in relationships.

When we meet someone of the opposite sex we usually put them in one of three categories – Yes, No, or Maybe. We all can find our No People in a lot less than ten minutes. Sleazy guys, liars, fakes, non-bathers, it's easy to put them in the No category and nobody would argue with that. The ones that go right into the Yes category are usually the ones who have outstanding physical charms that appeal to us. It's the Maybe category that I'm talking about. The person that might offer great possibilities if you give them a chance. What you need to do is not to move somebody from the Maybe category to the No category in ten minutes. Spend some more time in Maybeland and see how much fun it can be if you give it a chance.

The woman who takes the instant attraction route is dooming herself to failure. Often, attraction leads us to precisely the type of person we should avoid. The person seeking that "magic spark" is continually selecting only one type of man, and then complaining that all men are the same. Attraction is great and can lead to a lot of great, but meaningless, sex. Love, which is the basis of every solid relationship, is different from attraction. Love is based on deeper qualities than a person's eye color, shoulder width, and initial pick-up line.

Instead of picking out a guy, think about picking out a house. You look at ten or fifteen houses and then one instantly grabs your eye. A five-minute walk-though shows off a nice interior, but doesn't let you check out the basement. Do you immediately buy the house? Of course you don't; you're not an idiot. You check out the neighborhood, the price, the schools, and the utility bills. Then, you have a home inspection because you don't know what might be hiding behind those freshly painted walls. You're about to make a major investment so naturally you check it out thoroughly. You don't want to waste any time or money and get stuck with a lemon.

But you'll waste thousands of emotional dollars on dates because you are unable to be thorough, to look behind the initial impression when selecting potential partners. In fact, that initial impression becomes your guide for happiness. No spark, no follow-through. No chance to learn more about someone and no chance to learn more about yourself.

I'm not just speaking about appearance either, because I know that personality has a big influence on women's initial attraction (men are another story). What grabs your attention is not always what holds your attention. And just because it grabs your attention doesn't mean it's worthwhile. It's an axiom that you follow in every other area of life; why not follow it here too?

Let's apply the "instant spark" theory to buying clothes. When you're walking through Macys and you see an outfit that you love, do you immediately buy it? Nope. You look at the size, check the prices, examine it for defects, and then will try it on to see how it really fits. Just because it looks good on the rack doesn't mean it'll look good on you, so you've got to check to make sure that it doesn't make your thighs seem fat. You know that just because you're initially attracted to an outfit it's not necessarily something you want in your life. Why wouldn't the same be true for a relationship, which is a much more important item in your life?

Spending your dating career looking for "the spark" leads to two things. First, it ensures that you meet the same type of person every time, whether you're aware of it or not. The same person, incidentally, that you've proven won't be right for you because you're still single. If instant attraction led to successful relationships, you would be in one. Here's a quote that appeared later in the profile of one of our daters quoted above:

"I tried using this service about a year ago but never met anyone that I was attracted to. I want to meet some new people and seem to be in a rut with the same network of friends."

She openly admits that she's in a rut with meeting the same people, but doesn't see that it's because she is severely limiting herself. She never bothered to follow through with anyone on the service because she's looking for the magical "instant attraction." That's the real problem with looking for a spark; it's not based on anything real.

Real relationships are based on love, mutual respect, trust, and friendship. None of these characteristics can be determined in one quick meeting. People looking for "the spark" are really looking for someone who looks and behaves a specific way. That look or specific behavior has absolutely nothing to do with the person's actual personality. It usually has to do with the front that they put on to succeed in public and with women.

The personality that usually causes the instant spark is one of confidence and cockiness. You'll hear all the time from women that they want "someone confident, but not arrogant." Those are two qualities that are very difficult to separate, especially in men. Confidence is great, but it's nothing to build a relationship upon.

The confidence and arrogance that cause a man to make an initial dynamic impression are the same qualities that prevent him from ever being emotionally intimate. That's the second problem with "the spark." It seeks to replace true intimacy with attraction and the two are usually not related.

This whole syndrome is aggravated by Hollywood. There are dozens of movies, books, and TV shows where the arrogant, cocky man meets the gorgeous woman. There's an initial spark that both attracts and repels the woman. However, with the sheer force of her personality, the female star is able to convert the arrogant and good-looking jerk into a humbler, nicer man. **It doesn't happen in real life.**

In real life, the arrogant, cocky man continues to treat the woman in an arrogant and cocky manner. She wants him to be nicer, but he doesn't understand why the behavior that attracted her to him is suddenly wrong. The movie fantasy assumes that arrogance is caused by a lack of love and that by merely putting love into his life, the jerk becomes nice. Movie characters change because of a woman's love; real life characters stay the same, no matter how strong a woman's love. Character change takes significant, difficult, time-consuming work, not a bubble bath with Julia Roberts.

A Few Words About Speed Dating

This dating concept is spreading throughout the U.S. in the same way that the plague swept through Europe, with only slightly less disastrous results. Without a doubt, this is the absolute worst way to meet a quality date and it merely magnifies everything that's wrong with today's society and our inability to make lasting connections.

With this fee-based service, a large number of singles are crowded into a ballroom or some other generic hotel location. After a brief period of serving liquor in a vain attempt to disguise everyone's more obvious flaws, a signal is given and all of the men in the room sit down at their own table. Each woman is assigned a table and has a brief discussion with the slightly inebriated male denizen. Every five minutes, a bell is rung and, like Pavlov's dog, all of the women must move on to the next entrée in this buffet of desperation. Before you do, however, the man and the woman must write a "yes" or "no" next to an evaluation card. After about two hours, the cattle drive ends and the organizers tally up the results. If both people have written yes next to each other's name, then the organizers will provide contact information to each of them and the cycle of bad dates continues.

On the website of one of these "service" companies, the sideshow barkers from R____ Dating claim that this method will "help singles quickly connect in an upscale environment without all the pressure of the bar scene." Yes, meeting someone in a bar certainly has much more pressure than attempting to impress someone in a mere five-minute interview at a table in a hotel meeting room. At least if you find the person in a bar interesting, you can follow up with them if you desire. Not here, as soon as things start to get interesting, the bell forces you to move along Desperation Row.

That's right. You have all of five minutes of conversation to decide if this is the person with whom you want a relationship. Among the fabulous questions the organizers suggest you use to get conversation started is, "what excites you in life?", as if anyone is going to be able to answer this question in five minutes. Like asking, "what are your weaknesses?" during a job interview, your chances of getting an honest answer in this situation are remote.

Who does this process favor? The slick-talker, the used car salesman, and the person who excels at telling people what they want to hear. That's right, the exact person that you're desperately trying to get away from. It's a process that completely focuses on appearance and the superficial and unimportant aspects of a person's personality.

Let's take this concept away from the dating arena. Picture a five-minute job interview. You browse their résumé and ask one or two questions, but since you're unable to get in-depth with them on anything, you don't know what they did at each job and exactly what skills they possess. In a normal job interview, you ask a couple of questions, follow up their answers, and let them tell you their strengths and weaknesses while you compare that with their résumé and references. You can make an informed decision based on a true picture of the person. In a five-minute job interview, you are forced to make decisions on superficial items and you must take their résumé at face value. How often does that work out? Never, because I've never, ever been on a five-minute job interview, nor have I conducted one. No reputable company would conduct that kind of interview because the pitfalls are obvious. You would be laughed out of any company's Human Resources office for even suggesting such a thing. Yet hundreds of people are willing to base a decision **on their life partner** on this five minute chat. I spend more time picking out my socks. And I don't particularly like them.

Let's call this service what it really is, Cattle Call Dating. Take a number, check the teeth, mark your scorecard and move on. In-depth conversation? Forget it; busy professionals don't have time for that. After all, as the organizers blatantly state, "the first impression is a lasting one." Lasting - maybe, accurate - extremely doubtful. Let's face it; if you only needed five minutes to meet the right person, you wouldn't need to go to this service in the first place!

Take a minute and look at an ad for one of these services: *We started in April 2001 with a simple idea – to eliminate bad blind dates and Internet overload. R----- Dating makes it easy for people to know whether there's a connection in only 5 minutes! Let's face it... We save you time, money and frustration. At R----- Dating you know the people you're meeting are single, available, age-appropriate and looking to connect.*

Let's look at how they try and justify this ridiculous form of dating. By stressing the quantity of people at the service, as well as the "upscale" nature, the organizers are attempting to project an image of hundreds of desirable singles meeting. While I try to figure out exactly what's different about meeting in a hotel conference room or a hotel bar, let's examine some simple questions that need to be asked about speed dating.

What's so upscale about a hotel meeting room?

Is that any different than meeting in a hotel bar?

Does the ability to pay the $60 fee guarantee quality?

Is a five-minute conversation better than a blind date?

Is there any pre-screening to ensure quality people?

Is there any pre-screening to ensure that the people are

really single?

The answer to all of these questions is, of course, no. There is no way of telling who will show up to this event and the only thing people have to do to qualify is pay the entrance fee. They can usually ensure quantity, but we all know that's a far cry from quality. If you want a quantity of men paying attention to you, wear an extremely low-cut blouse. Neither option ensures quality, just browsers interested in your physicality.

Here's what the most amazing thing about Cattle Call Dating. When I looked at making a reservation, most events are already booked solid with female participants. That's right, females, not males, are the most eager to try this out. The same sex that is constantly complaining about the superficial nature of relationships and men is the very same one which is clamoring to make five-minute judgments on the person they want to spend the rest of their life with.

When I mention my objections to this type of dating to my female friends, they all give me the same response; "It's great because I can tell I don't want to date somebody right away." One friend added, "if a person comes up and he's into dancing at clubs, I know that I can eliminate him right away because that's not right for me." She's right; it is easy to eliminate the obvious non-contenders in five minutes. You don't need rapid dating to do that, however, it's obvious whenever you meet the undateable. It's also easy to find the obvious contenders, mainly because they stick out like a sore thumb. However, this kind of dating eliminates that middle range person, the one who doesn't make a tremendously strong first impression. It gets rid of them because it encourages you to place the person that doesn't *immediately* turn you on into the "not willing to date" pile.

By encouraging you to make a decision in five minutes, speed dating actually creates the completely wrong dynamic by forcing you to look for reasons **not** to like somebody. In that time period, only a superficial view is presented, so you must pick superficial things to eliminate the other person. You can't learn about honesty, a sense of humor, trust, or decency in five minutes, so you make judgments based on whether or not the person likes skiing. As all of my female friends said above, "I can tell that I don't want to date a person in five minutes," so their thought process is based on elimination. It's American Idol for spouses and everybody is Simon. In order to make speed dating work, you have to think "do I see any obvious personality flaws?" not "why would I want a guy who doesn't like to ride bikes?"

Think of all of the people whom you've met in your life. How many of them made a great first impression? Now think of all of the times that you've met somebody and not given your best impression. Does it mean that that experience turned out badly? Of course it doesn't. I've done a lot of job interviews and I know that the person who often gives the best first impression is not always the best person for the job. That's why job interviews take longer than five minutes; you need more time than that to learn anything of substance. You need time to see behind the façade we all present in initial encounters and see the real person. By tossing all but the slickest out, you're missing out on a ton of high quality people, one of who might be everything you're looking for in a life partner.

Guideline #4

Movies are not Good Role Models

Or

Hookers Never Look Like Julia Roberts

Hollywood, in its quest for happy endings, constantly feeds people the absolute wrong messages with their movies. I've touched in this briefly in earlier chapters, but let me reinforce that with a few facts that directly contradict most movies:

- People do not fall in love with other people whom they hate at first sight. They just wind up hating them even more.

- Mean guys, jerks, and criminals do not become nice, upstanding citizens because of a woman's love. Instead they drag the woman down with them.

- Criminals are scum, the lowest form of life on earth and are not charming, fun and exciting dates that should be idolized. They take things they didn't earn.

- Children are never, ever able to get their parents matched up.

- Dangerous men do not make good husbands. I can just hear Mrs. Indiana Jones now, "Running off to find the Holy Grail was fine when you were young, but when are you going to stop fooling around with those old pots and start helping me with the kids?"

- Nice guys are not always boring and dating one is not "settling."

- Being kidnapped by terrorists does not change your feelings about a man, even if he does rescue you by flying a Harrier jet up the terrorist's ass.

- Men don't act like jerks because they haven't found the right woman. They act like jerks because they're jerks.

Let me give a few comments on some popular movies about relationships and let you know how they're steering you wrong.

French Kiss

I like both stars, but the message of this movie is terrible. Somehow Meg Ryan is going to find happiness with a cruel French thief instead of a steady, nice guy? Women think it's romantic for some reason, but it's a reminder to us nice guys of how we're constantly belittled in the media. In this movie, she and the thief end up together and you're left to assume a life of happiness for them, when in reality a thief is a thief, not a person you'd want to associate with. A person who steals and thinks it's okay is not able to magically become a great guy to his wife because the same personality flaws that allow him to steal will also cause him to be a jerk to his wife. Think about it for one minute. A thief is somebody who makes a living by taking from people who work for their things. That's somebody you want to make a life with? That's somebody to be idolized? Think of how you felt in the third grade when somebody stole the Hostess Twinkie from your lunch –

that's how a thief deliberately makes people feel every day. In other words, great husband material, right?

Music and Lyrics

I have to preface this by saying that I love this movie, even though it has a terrible message for relationships. We'll flash forward towards the end of the movie when Drew Barrymore is asking her sister how you know when the guy loves you for you. Her answer is, "when he does something exceptional." Really? Something exceptional is how you define true love? So, of course, Hugh Grant botches the relationship and redeems himself by performing a song he wrote to a sold out concert at Madison Square Garden that just happens to include Barrymore and her sister in the audience. During the song's performance, Barrymore's sister looks over at her and gives her a grin meaning, "See, he just did something exceptional so you know that he loves you." She immediately forgives him all his sins and runs backstage to make out with him.

Now I don't know about you, but the chances to do something exceptional don't often occur in my life, even when I look for them. I have never had a former love who has been held hostage and needed rescuing, nor do I have a job that allows me to box for the world championship, rescue a drowning kayaker in cold Alaskan waters, or get on TV to make a dramatic statement. I'm also pretty sure if I got up to sing during a concert at Madison Square Garden that I would be ruthlessly pummeled by security, which would not impress any woman. The big dramatic gestures popularized by Hollywood are completely impossible for most of us. Shows like *The Bachelor* make it worse because they provide money and support personnel that allow supposedly ordinary people to have dramatic moments and women tend to expect them more and more.

Doing something dramatic in the real world doesn't happen. Public declarations of love and regret get laughed at, not rewarded. A person shows you that he loves you for you by treating you well and loving you without reservation. When someone makes a mistake, forgiveness shouldn't require a hostage rescue, just understanding.

You've Got Mail

Another great misdirection movie. Tom Hanks destroys Meg Ryan's livelihood, yet she's able to forgive him and fall in love with him. How many times have you really pissed off a woman and had her forgive you, let alone fall in love with you? I'm guessing it's about the same number of times I've had sex with Elle MacPherson. Women get mad if you don't like a meal they cook, let alone if you try and destroy their business. The anger, contempt, and condescension Hanks shows Ryan would not magically turn to love for her and his plans for her business wouldn't change because she has great eyes and is a great kisser. Plus, a guy who ruthlessly tries to eliminate his competitor is not a nice guy. Hanks is such a great actor that he makes that character believable and likeable, but a guy who is a jerk in business is a jerk in real life as well.

Thelma and Louise

The number one angry chick flick. I love how Susan Sarandon convinces Geena Davis that the cops will never buy the self-defense story. Yeah, abused women never get off with stopping their attacker. Of course they do and cops are more sensitive than ever to that subject. Hell, people get off murder charges all the time. Women who stop an attacker end up on Oprah and the subject of a glowing Lifetime movie. Women will say that because Geena Davis was an abused wife, she didn't how to react properly when she was attacked. That's true, but they don't take that argument to its logical conclusion which is that Susan Sarandon also abuses Geena, by playing on her weaknesses and fears. What her character does to Geena Davis' character is just as abusive as the husband she's fleeing. Actually, it's worse because she convinces Davis that there's no hope and that death is the only option. Women would be appalled if Sarandon's character gave

Davis a bunch of pills to take to kill herself, but that's no different than convincing her to drive off a cliff.

Angry women love this movie because all of the men are jerks and treat women badly. What a horrible message, especially because they leave out the fact that nobody forced Geena Davis to marry a loser or to have sex with a drifter. That's a smart move, by the way, having sex in a motel with a strange guy whom you picked up hitchhiking! We're supposed to be surprised that he stole her money? We're supposed to feel sorry for her because she was abused by another man? Yes, she was, but she's an adult who deliberately and consistently made bad decisions. Did she deserve the bad things that happened to her? Of course not, but who does? That's not a license to continue to allow bad things to happen to you.

The real problem here is that Geena Davis' character is unable to trust anyone and that was true before the drifter screwed her. She married a guy that she didn't trust and she doesn't trust law enforcement to do the right thing because everybody that's a man is untrustworthy. Then, to show those awful, abusive men, the women kill themselves? That's something to admire? Ridiculous.

In real life, the women would surrender and become media darlings. A hot-shot lawyer would take their case for free and it'd be plastered all over Court TV. After getting a slap on the wrist, the women would become rich with their own Lifetime movie and giving speeches to angry women all over the country.

Gone With the Wind

An excellent movie that attempts to turn a "chick flick" into a guy movie by having a war take place in the middle. The heroine, whom we're supposed to fall in love with, spends a lot of the movie scheming to steal her sister's husband. Well, that's admirable.

When Scarlett finds a man to marry, Clark Gable manages to make a violent and abusive man into a sympathetic character. Let's see, the message there is that a woman who "acts up" can be brought around to love if you physically and mentally dominate her. There's a nice message.

Finally, when the hero decides that Scarlett has been such a bitch that even hitting her can't relieve his stress, he leaves. Somehow, we're supposed to believe that Scarlett finds immense strength in his leaving and turns her life around. In reality, Scarlett would simply find another abusive jerk to marry.

Pretty Woman

Ahh, the king of all girl movies. I'll dispense with the usual argument about how prostitution is nothing like it's portrayed here because this is a movie; they're allowed to take some liberties with reality. The real problem is how the relationship between Richard Gere and Julia Roberts develops.

First off, guys that have been ignored and abandoned by their dads don't suddenly become warm, loveable guys because they fall in love. They certainly don't open up to a woman merely because she looks good in a red dress. Richard Gere's character's problems are so deep that he would need years of therapy to treat

any woman as anything but an object. He even mentions how it

took years of therapy to admit he hated his father, but that therapy

apparently didn't teach him how to be a decent human being.

Secondly, Julia Roberts would have had far more serious

problems than she lets on to wind up a prostitute on the streets of

Hollywood Boulevard doing tricks for $100. Psychologists will tell

us that most street walkers were abused in childhood and this is

one way that trauma comes out as an adult. You don't spend

months on the streets, sleeping with any schmo for fifty bucks and

magically become a princess. There would be a ton of hatred and

resentment towards men deep inside her that would prevent any

such relationship from happening. It would also force her to

sabotage the relationship if it approached even a slight level of

intimacy.

Now I know that it's only a movie and that I'm being too

literal. However, millions of women watch this movie repeatedly

and they do believe that their love can make a rotten guy into a good guy. People do not change without extensive therapy and hard work and this movie makes the exact opposite point. Unfortunately, women make allowances for the prostitution portion being unrealistic, but not the romantic part. By doing that, they are encouraged to get involved with men that they have no way of changing.

Guideline #5

There's no Such Thing as a Jerk Magnet

Or

All Men Aren't Jerks

Women have complained about this role for eons, but it was given voice by Julia Roberts' character in "Pretty Woman." She is explaining to Richard Gere why she became a prostitute and she briefly describes a series of horrible boyfriends. Roberts ends the recitation with a slight laugh, saying, "My mom used to call me a bum magnet," as if it is her boyfriends' fault that she became a prostitute.

The Jerk Magnet is an amazingly popular role for women. Entire books and talk shows have been created to explain away this phenomenon, or even better, blame it all on men. Another name for this role could be the Martyr, as Jerk Magnets will spend endless hours with their girlfriends discussing the different ways in which their boyfriends have been jerks.

The sob story of Jerk Magnets is quite familiar to Oprah watchers and usually has at least two of the items on the following list of complaints:

He just shows up at my place late at night and wants sex.

When he's with his friends, it's like I don't even exist.

He spends more time with his friends than me.

His car gets more attention than I do.

I went and got my hair, nails, and make-up done and he didn't even notice.

He forgot our anniversary/my birthday/Valentine's Day.

After sex, he never cuddles; he just turns on the TV or falls asleep.

He never calls me in advance or makes plans, he just expects me to be there for him.

Call me? Forget it; I always have to call him.

Sound familiar? I'm sure it does to all of you, especially women. In fact, if you go to the supermarket and check out the latest edition of Cosmo, you'll see a cover blurb about the latest innocent woman falling prey to the mean, evil, jerk man. Here's a newflash for you: if you're dating jerks, it's **YOUR** fault for picking jerks. It's not their fault for being jerks. They were jerks before you dated them, they'll be jerks while they're dating you, and they'll be jerks after they've dumped you.

That's right; it's your fault for dating the jerk because you're the one that picked him out. He was probably rude or arrogant to you when you first met. That's one of the signs of jerks; they're almost completely unable to hide being a jerk. Jerks are jerks because they just cannot stop doing the irritating, rude, and stupid things that define jerkdom.

If you talk to your friends or anyone else who knows the guy, they will all say that he's a jerk. Some of his friends will even tell you that "he may seem like a jerk, but once you get to know him he's really cool." His co-workers will describe him as a jerk and if you're in school, so will his teachers. He may occasionally be funny, nice, or even smart, but all of those characteristics are drowned out by his being a jerk. In fact, if you look back to your first discussions of him with your friends, they will have said that he's a jerk. Or you will have felt that he was a jerk to others, but he is "nice to me."

In fact, he may be friendly to you, but he's not nice to you. More importantly, if he's friendly only to you, that's a horrible sign. A person that treats everyone poorly, or those who are not his "buds" poorly, is a bad person. Period. End of discussion. Look at how a person treats those around him and you'll have a very good indication of how he will be treating you at some point in your relationship. Open up your eyes and look at how the guy speaks to you, his friends, and waitresses, especially female ones.

Since Jerk Magnets don't seem to realize that jerks are jerks until they've had a ton of sex with them, here are some ways of realizing that a guy is a jerk.

His car has a stereo system worth more than $3,000.

He drives a Hummer.

He's been arrested (not convicted, just arrested, that's all it takes).

He doesn't have friends, he has "buds."

He owns more gold chains than you.

He calls his child "the kid."

He likes big dogs and doesn't like cats or other animals.

His sunglasses cost more than $300.

His money is stored in a money clip, not a wallet.

He has more than three tattoos, or one tattoo that covers 10% of his body area.

His favorite sports teams are the New York Yankees and the Dallas Cowboys.

He still thinks it's really fun to go out and "get wasted."

You may think that the Jerk Identification List is pretty humorous, or at least I hope you do, but it's meant as more than a joke list. Those are real signs of a jerk. Look at them for a minute and you can realize that they describe someone narcissistic and mainly concerned with himself and his needs. That's a perfect definition of a jerk. Anybody who presents more than three of these symptoms is going to be trouble at some point in the relationship.

After showing this list to a friend of mine, she asked if it works for girls too. After giving it some thought, I just can't say yes. I can't think of any woman who is a jerk, it's exclusively a male thing. Women do not have that combination of testosterone, arrogance, stupidity and self-absorption it takes to be jerks. Women can be bitchy, but that implies a little more intelligence than your basic jerk. Jerkdom goes beyond that. At the heart of every jerk is a scared little person with no self-confidence. Women who don't have self-confidence usually have the common decency not to take it out on others and instead develop an eating disorder.

The woman without self-confidence never develops into a jerk, leaving jerkdom solely a male domain.

Guideline #6

Keep Your Weirdness to Yourself at First

Or

Don't You Understand How Odd That is?

We all have our own hobbies or theories that are not mainstream ones. It's part of what makes each person unique and isn't necessarily a bad thing. It might be something simple like running a Get Smart website (me) or something more complex like dressing up as a Klingon and going to Star Trek conventions. As with anything unusual, however, it's best not to lead with that when introducing yourself to a person. You don't have to hide it and deliberately create a fake person, but let's save the part where you dress up like a fairy and pretend to fly at fairy conventions until to I get to know you a for little bit. If you lead with that, then you become the Fairy Girl, not Janice who happens to have an unusual hobby. I think what's happened is that as our society has become more narcissistic, we have lost our ability to see ourselves as others see us. We start to believe that everybody believes what we believe. We think that our reality is the reality of everyone else. Far from it.

Think of your first date or first meeting as the first day of your trial. Would you go to court dressed in baggy jeans and a torn t-shirt? Would you refuse to stand up when the judge tells everyone to rise? Would you speak only in Klingon? Of course you wouldn't. You want to make a good impression, or at least a not bad one. You want the judge to take you seriously and believe you and have faith in you and you do that by conforming to some basic norms of society. Use a little of the same discretion on an initial meeting.

For example, I was on a first date with Cynthia, an attractive girl of around my age. We were having a nice dinner at a Middle Eastern restaurant when the conversation took a slight turn into the Twilight Zone.

"I'm not happy to just sit around and watch TV or hang out at the house," Cynthia said. "I like to be out doing stuff all the time."

"What do you like to do?" I replied.

This seemingly innocuous and natural question was immediately met with silence and a glare not seen since Jack Webb was interrogating hippies on *Dragnet*. After an incredibly long and silent thirty seconds, her tightly pressed lips formed a harsh rejoinder.

"What do you mean, what do I like to do?" she snarled.

"You just said you like to be out doing stuff," I replied nervously. "I just wanted to know what kind of stuff you like to do for fun. You know… hobbies and things." At this point, I was completely baffled. The question of what do you do for fun is one of the most common first date questions. We've all been asked that a thousand times. How in the world could somebody be upset or offended that I asked her what her hobbies were, especially after she just brought up that she had a lot of hobbies?

"I like to do a lot of stuff, but one thing I love to do, and my girlfriends think I'm crazy, but I love to go to the shooting range and take target practice. Guys are always amazed that I'm such a great shot and that I love to shoot. Most of them are lucky to get one or two shots in the body, but I can empty an entire clip right in the heart. In fact, my ex wouldn't let me keep a gun in the house because he was afraid I'd kill him," Cynthia added with a laugh.

Here's another newsflash for you. It's not a good idea to mention on a first date that previous boyfriends feared that you would shoot them! It's an even worse idea to let out a laugh as you mention that fact. Boldly stating that your ex was someone worth killing and that you could kill someone are not strong points. It's not the shooting part that's bizarre, although you might want to save that one for later in the relationship, but laughing about killing your boyfriend is quite scary.

I was on another first date with a woman named Anne. She was either a nurse or a linebacker for the Dallas Cowboys – with her build I wasn't sure. We were having a normal conversation when she brought up the fact that she doesn't have a large shoe collection. Since that's like a guy saying he has never watched any porn, I followed up by asking a few more questions. Anne then discussed how she had to get rid of her old boyfriend because he had a foot fetish and the final straw was when she caught him masturbating in her shoes (bonus points if you didn't look at your shoes after reading this). Now how do you follow up that story? It changes the whole mood of the night. Odd sexual stories belong in Penthouse, not on a first date.

What needs to take place on the first meeting is getting an understanding of the core of the person. You're not going to learn everything or even most things, but you'll get a decent feel for the person. After you've established yourself as a non-psychotic person you can start to bring out your unusual hobbies. Let's go back to my website example. I've run a fan website for the TV show *Get Smart* since 1995. It's a fun hobby and it's given me a lot of pleasure, but I also realize that the general impression of people who run fan websites is that of a fat, anti-social guy who lives in his parents' basement. They think we're all like Comic Book Guy on *The Simpsons*. So I don't bring up the website until I've already made an impression of a non-supernerd. Let the person accept the good and decent core person you are and then they can see how whatever unusual hobby or interest you have fits into that picture. Whatever you establish first in their minds will be the way they define you for a long time. So establish sanity first and then reveal you have a complete Imperial Stormtrooper uniform in your closet.

Hey, I'm Nuts!

Not everyone is able to understand that they might be unusual or that they're advertising themselves as nuts. It's actually quite easy to see when a person is nuts and someone you might want to stay away from. A great place to see that is in dating profiles because everything you write and believe says something about you. In fact, you can tell a lot about a person by just a few lines, though it's usually not what the writer intended, as what many people think is a positive is actually a negative. Here are some word-for-word statements that I've picked out from dating websites. Underneath, I've placed my translation of their ad, in the hopes that people will gain some self-knowledge and learn to avoid appearing nuts.

I am a 42 year old female that is independent, emotionally secure and knows who I am. I am seeking a man that is not intimidated by this.

"I'm a tremendous pain in the ass." She likes to believe that she scares men away because she "knows who I am." She really drives men away because by "knowing who she is," she refuses to compromise or adjust to meet the needs of others. Men are not intimidated by emotionally secure women, in fact, we love them. Men hate ball-busters that make demands, who are so sure of themselves and their beliefs that they are unable to take anyone else's feelings into account. We feel about them the exact same way women feel about arrogant men.

Love , Respect and Honesty. I'm still hanging on the thought that there are men like that out there.

I always pick losers and users. There are plenty of men like that out there, but I won't date them because I'm always looking for the exciting, dangerous guy. If I had a nice guy, I wouldn't know what to do with him. In fact, I'd probably start acting out, hoping to drive him away.

I'll also be honest and say that I'm looking for a certain physical type: tall, non-balding, young-looking, and conventionally handsome.

I'm shallow and if you don't look exactly like my dream guy, I won't hear a word you say or even bother to look for your good points. Is anyone surprised that she's 39 and never married? And if a guy put in his profile that he was looking for a "conventionally beautiful" woman, most women would be offended and ignore him.

The type of guy I'm looking for is adventuresome, but not reckless; highly masculine, but not chauvinistic; and in shape and active, but not into watching sports and doesn't live in a gym.

I'm looking for Indiana Jones, a fictional character. An active, in-shape man who doesn't like sports or working out? There are maybe three straight guys in every city who have that kind of genetics, none over the age of thirty. Active guys love sports, that's what starts us being active and you can't separate what you like from what you don't like in the same activity. The Star Trek nerd explanation is to think of the episode where Captain Kirk split into two beings, one all-good and one all-bad. They couldn't exist without each other. For the non-nerd explanation - life is not a Chinese buffet where you pick out one item from each column that you like and can completely ignore some things that you don't like. In relationships, sometimes you have to eat a little spinach to have a steak.

I've been told I need a man with a strong personality, which is most likely true, given that I have a strong one myself.

I'm a bitch.

I realize that my priorities are changing a lot now. Where I used to spend a lot of my time and energy on my career, I'm beginning to focus more on my friends, families, and relationships.

I'm in my late thirties and want kids. The memories of all of those people whom I've treated badly and ignored in the pursuit of my selfish need for power and materialistic things are haunting me. I've learned that success is only good when you have a loving partner to share it with.

Bonus points for owning one of the following forms of transportation: motorcycle, speedboat, convertible, private jet.

I like the bad boys and fast cars, as I'm more interested in what you do then who you are. The thrills of speed and money compensate for my inability to be truly intimate with someone, at least for now. I'll be spending the next few years dating bad boys and complaining about how they don't listen or pay attention to my needs.

tigrrrrr and lily, though the big cat probably is predominant and the other accessed more when i know and trust someone.

I'm a nut.

Will give until it hurts, but looking for someone who will give back.

I really got hurt by my last boyfriend, an emotionally unavailable guy. I'm also a little co-dependent, as you shouldn't have to give until it hurts. It should be hard, but it shouldn't hurt.

Firstly, let me say that I HAVE NO TOLERANCE FOR DRUGS!!!

I've dated a lot of addicts/alcoholics, even though they didn't seem like they were like that at first. My father was an addict and I've never gotten any treatment for growing up like that, so I keep picking guys just like "dear old dad."

If I spend a few years in ALANON, I might be a great

catch, but I'm still blaming the problem on the guys I date,

not the fact that I pick them.

I will say that I am addicted to adrenaline - I love riding

motorcycles (I used to own a Kawasaki Ninja) and would someday

like to take up skydiving.

I use adrenaline to replace intimacy. My happiness comes

from external stimulation, not the true intimacy that a

relationship requires. If I date a nice man, I'll berate him

for being dull.

I am not: a bimbo, a drunk, a chameleon, a snoop, an athlete, or

ordinary.

I have behaved like all of the above at some time and now

I'm shocked when people treat me like that. I have

absolutely no self-awareness and I'm surprised and bitter

when people treat me according to the way I behave because I think I'm doing nothing wrong.

You'll be at least ONE of these things: a tennis pro, a tennis player, a tennis partner, a tennis vacation partner, tennis tournament attendee, or a TV tennis match watching partner.

I'm way, way too involved in tennis (substitute any activity here). Obsession is never good and focusing only on people who are addicted to tennis or any other sport is ridiculous. Let me turn this around. Take that sentence and replace "tennis" with "Star Trek." You'd run screaming, right? There is absolutely no difference between the two statements, except for the condition of the elbow of the person making it. Tennis may be healthy, but obsessing over it sure isn't.

I hope you're tall, with dark hair and blue eyes (like Lord Aragorn) -- oh wait, that's just in my dreams. [Note: the 'tall' part is pretty important to me, so if you happen to be under 5'10" and the perfect

man, I'll probably miss out; because I probably will not respond to

your ever so enticing emails]

I'm not sure who Lord Aragorn is, but I'm quite sure he's not somebody that I'd mention in a personal ad, especially at our age. Fantasy is nice, but reality is reality. This one would be sad if it weren't so irritating. Imagine openly stating that you'd pass up the perfect man because he's not 5'10". Wow. If a guy wrote an ad stating that women with a cup size under "C" shouldn't respond, he'd be openly lynched, and rightfully so. Not only that, but can you imagine what would happen if some guy dumped her because she wasn't physically perfect (and I can guarantee you she isn't)? The person who wrote this was 37 years old and she still hasn't learned that what's inside is most important.

Sociology, philosophy, literature, pop culture, psychology, social

issues, etc. interest me, though sometimes I enjoy people more in

theory than in practice! I prefer one-on-one situations to being

herded with the masses.

I'm not popular, have very few friends, and I'm convinced

that I'm superior to all of you. I need one-on-one situations

because I'm so annoying that I've never had more than one

friend. I like to blame my aloneness on how dumb and

shallow most people are, but it's really because I'm

condescending and nasty to people. Deep down I just want

to be liked. I'm not, so I'm bitter, which reinforces my

aloneness.

Guideline #7

Arrogance is NOT a Good Trait

Or

What Women Really Want

If you read any polls or surveys about what women want in a mate, two things always come to the top of the list – a sense of humor and confidence. I'll deal with the sense of humor subject later, but let's take a look at confidence. It is a wonderful trait and it absolutely is one that women look for. However, there are a lot of shades of gray when talking about confidence and that perfect balance of self-confidence and humbleness is especially tough to find. Let's illustrate this with the mountain of self-confidence:

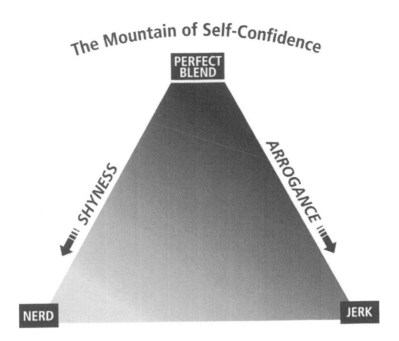

The Mountain of Self-Confidence

PERFECT BLEND

SHYNESS

ARROGANCE

NERD

JERK

At the top of the mountain is the perfect blend of self-confidence and humility. It's a pretty small apex and I'm sure you'll all agree that most people fall on either side of the perfect blend. On the left side, or the side you climb to reach self-confidence, is the quiet, shy, and slightly insecure person. The farther down the side you get the more insecure you are until you reach the bottom – nerd. On the other side of self-confidence is arrogance and it goes all the way down until the bottom – jerk.

Both sides of the mountain feature people with self-confidence, with it getting stronger as you get towards the top of the mountain. The problem comes because women confuse quietness with weakness, arrogance with strength. In fact, the reverse is true because the arrogant male is using arrogance to cover up his weaknesses. These weaknesses usually become apparent after four-six months of dating, when the woman he's dating starts to complain about him to The Nice Guy.

A touch of arrogance is good; it's what ensured the survival of the human race for generations. The arrogant guy would lead the group against the wooly mammoth and be able to defend his mate much better. It's natural that throughout history women are genetically drawn to the arrogant male, as it was their best chance for survival. Arrogance is a trait that will help a person accumulate power and career success. As humanity has matured, those traits now are the ones that destroy relationships. The arrogance that led him to go against all odds and attack the saber toothed tiger now lead him to go skiing with his buddies on the weekend he was supposed to spend with you and your parents.

Arrogance is not a synonym for self-confidence. In fact, it's only those few at the top of the mountain who have both. Arrogance generally means the absence of self-confidence. Since there is no self-confidence, the person is unable to be truly intimate, which he covers up by being arrogant, ignoring the needs of those around him. Since he is unable to be intimate, he uses his arrogance to assert himself first, which translates into selfishness. You'll then hear their girlfriend discuss how he's never thinking of her. Of course not! The arrogant guy is unable to think of anybody else. It's how he succeeds in business – he always puts himself first.

On the other side of the mountain, we have the quiet guy, who is always ignored by women. While Jerk is at the bottom of the arrogant side of the pyramid, Nerd is at the bottom of the quiet side of the pyramid. The people on this side replace their lack of self-confidence with shyness. As you go up that side towards self-confidence, what you find is strength. True strength of character does not require arrogance to illustrate it to others. Truly self-confident men do not have to tell people they're self-confident. It's obvious in everything they do. The quiet self-confident man is secure enough in himself to accept others and be truly intimate, which is really every woman's dream.

A lot of women realize that arrogance is not self-confidence, at least intellectually. Read any ten personal ads and you'll find at least five women who want a guy "who is self-confident but not arrogant." However, that woman is speaking from the experience of dating a lot of arrogant guys, that's how she knows enough to separate arrogance. She has always gone to the right side of the pyramid. Let's take a look at a revised version of the Mountain of Self-Confidence. I call it, the Mountain of Sex.

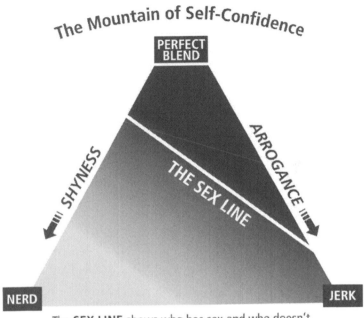

The **SEX LINE** shows who has sex and who doesn't, with those on the right side of the line getting sex.

That's the real problem here; women will unhesitatingly go towards the right side of the pyramid and reward the people on that side of the pyramid with sex. I have had many wonderful women friends and just about every one of them has had a one-night stand or brief fling with a guy and every single time it's with somebody on the right side of the pyramid. We even celebrate that in movies and books. So much so that you'll see many comedy movies where the punch line is an attractive woman having sex with a nerd. Though the power and initial strength of the arrogant person are appealing at first, the arrogance prevents any real relationship. A good relationship requires giving, receiving, and being truly intimate, none of which the arrogant man can offer. Women generally realize this after a little bit of time in the relationship and will leave, complaining about the number of arrogant men in the world. Well, why shouldn't we behave in an arrogant fashion? Those are the guys that get laid.

What women need to do is err on the left side of the mountain. While the down slope of the right side of the mountain is arrogance; the down slope of the left side of the mountain is quiet. Quiet guys who have a little bit of self-confidence are a thousand times more giving than arrogant guys with a little bit of self-confidence. Plus, since women ignore their side of the mountain, quiet guys are much more grateful and more willing to do things for the woman.

I've had a lot of women argue this point with me, saying that they often go to the quiet side. Here's how you can tell if you have or not. Think of all of the guys you've had sex with. Think how many of them were jerks or arrogant. Think how many of them were quiet guys or nerds. I'm pretty sure I know which end of the pyramid you're going to be on.

One final thought. If you're going to date someone who's arrogant, don't be surprised when that arrogance gets turned back on you.

Guideline #8

I Want a Guy With a Sense of Humor?

Or

No I Don't

Every few months, one of those lovely women's magazines like *Cosmo* or *Vogue* will come out with a survey heralding "What Women Really Want!" Universally, the trait that tops the lists is a sense of humor. Those of us with great senses of humor don't find that funny at all, as no woman is actually attracted to a sense of humor. What that really means is that women want the arrogant guy they're dating to have a sense of humor, which he usually doesn't.

The proof is simple; take a look at the dating patterns that are established in high school and college. There's a funny guy in every class. Did you ever see women flocking to him, trying to pick him up? Of course you didn't. They'll talk to him, but when it comes to dating, they're off with the arrogant guy almost every time. Did you ever see a poster of Steve Martin or John Candy in a woman's dorm room in college? There are a lot more posters of that gay guy from Twilight in girls' bedrooms than of Will Ferrell. That pattern, though lessened somewhat with age, still remains a vital component of dating.

If you are a funny guy, you also then get into trouble because men and women have fundamentally different senses of humor, men have one. What many women find appalling many men find funny. That's why we watched *Porky's* 27 times while you all were in the theatre next door crying over *The Piano*.

Here are some things that men find funny:

Body noises, both ours and other peoples

Other people's injuries

Enemies failing

Friends failing

Physical violence

The Marx Brothers

The Circus

Here are some things that women find funny:

Men doing stupid things

Chaucer

A sense of humor is something that women intellectually want and know is good, but fail to convert into action. A boring, handsome guy will get four times as many dates as a funny, average looking guy.

As an experiment, I joined an online dating service and wrote a funny ad describing myself. I used a funny headline and my regular picture and as you can tell, I'm an average looking guy. Not Don Johnson, but a nice, solid seven. Here's the ad:

I'm a great catch – cute, funny, smart, nice, honest, and a good cook to boot. It's so hard to sell yourself in one of these ads, but I'd like to give you the Top Ten Reasons You Should E-Mail Me

1. I've never been featured on America's Most Wanted.

2. I have a good job that I enjoy.

3. My shirt and pants match over sixty percent of the time.

4. I make incredibly good brownies and I clean the dishes afterwards.

5. I have far more hair on my head than my back.

6. I listen.

7. I rarely need to stay home and watch "the game."

8. I stop and ask for directions. I don't follow them, but at least I stop and ask for them.

9. I get along with all of my relatives, including my parents.

10. I don't mind spending three hours with you in the mall as we search for the perfect pair of shoes.

Now the jokes aren't the greatest, but I read the ad to several female friends and they all laughed. Not all of them were just being nice either; they would have clearly told me if my jokes were horrible, as they love to point out my failings. What was the result of the ad? Despite 56 people viewing my profile, not a single woman wrote to me. I also initiated contact with eleven women, sending them my profile, but the result was the same, an empty Inbox. Three months later, I switched my username and picture, this time using the headshot of a good looking friend of mine who lived across the country. The rest of the ad was exactly the same. I received seventeen e-mail approaches in the three days before I took the ad down. Two of them were from women I had written to with the old ad but who never responded to it. Women like a sense of humor, but they want it to be inside a handsome person.

I Can't Stand You – I Must Have You!

One of the most popular online dating services is eHarmony. Theoretically, it uses a special set of "29 points" to create couples, providing you with "an ideal match." In reality, they don't explain their process and they're free to match you up with whomever they want. In fact, the number of matches you will receive from them magically doubles or triples in the week before your membership lapses, leading one to wonder whether it's a scientific approach or a marketing approach that creates matches.

One of the central tenets of eHarmony is the Must Have/Can't Stand List. What they do is present a huge list of traits and you must pick ten things that you "must have" in your partner and ten things that you "can't stand" in your partner. While a good idea on the surface, absolutely none of the traits mentioned has any bearing in real relationships. What they do with this list is give you a ton of abstract principles that would be great if you were writing a play, but do not stand up to real world relationships. It's like how Superman always wanted "truth, justice, and the American way." Everybody wants that, but we all define it a little differently. It also plays right into the idealized image of a mate that women have been carrying around with them. The Must Have/Can't Stand list is so artificially generic it's like reading a horoscope.

Here are some of the highlights from their list of Must Haves and Can't Stands, along with my version of how it should be in the real dating world.

The eHarmony Must Haves.

Chemistry...

I must feel deeply in love with and attracted to my partner.

Sigh. Is there really anyone seeking a relationship that doesn't have this as a must have? Okay, Paris Hilton, but anybody else? This is part of their "unique system" of matching people, to say that that each partner should be deeply in love with one another? What the hell else is there? Who wouldn't check this one off? And when is this supposed to happen? On the first date? The mastermind of eHarmony says that you should know whether or not you're right for each other after two dates. Two dates? Ridiculous. Granted, it's pretty easy to spot the obvious mismatches after two minutes, but by telling people that they only need two dates to know who's right for them, you're encouraging the very superficial behavior that you denigrate.

Carl's Rephrase: I must feel a growing love and attraction to my partner, one which evolves and flourishes over time.

Communicator...

I must have someone who is good at talking and listening.

A good trait and nice to check off, but it's also unrealistic. Think of all of the people you know who are good at talking – are any of them good listeners? Of course they're not. Do all of them think that they're good listeners? Of course they do. Let's get even more brutally honest – how many men want a woman who is good at talking? Especially because they always want to talk right as the two-minute warning sounds? We want a woman who knows when not to talk, but, since that's realistic, it's nowhere on this list.

Carl's Rephrase: I must have someone who knows when to talk and when to listen and is good at both.

Verbal Intimacy...
I must know that my partner is sharing their deepest emotional thoughts and desires.

There are two problems with this one and I bet you already know what I'm going to say about it. No man wants to constantly share his deepest thoughts and desires, even if he's aware of them. Women are always trying to "share" and search for our deep thoughts, but men are instinctual and rarely examine their own thoughts, which aren't that deep and that's the second problem. Men don't have or want the same deep thoughts that women have.

Aside from a few gay philosophers and stoners over the ages, men don't have or search for deep thoughts. This continually puzzles women, which is why it appears several places in this book. When we say that we're thinking of nothing, **we're thinking of nothing**! We don't analyze for ulterior motives, we don't plan for the future. We're instinctual creatures who are primarily concerned with sex, food, and sports. Yes, we spend more time thinking about the Raiders quarterback situation than our deepest desire for happiness, but that's because solving the Raiders quarterback situation is our deepest desire for happiness.

Here's an example. It's an office workplace and there's a new temp worker who happens to be an attractive female. She spends three days at work and is friendly, talking to everybody. In addition, she wears professional, but sexy clothes. At the end of her third day at this new workplace, all of the other women in that workplace will be analyzing the temp's every move, from whom she talks with to how she reacts to the tasks she performs, instantly assuming that the woman has an ulterior motive for every single thing she says to a permanent worker. At the end of the third day, the men in the workplace are still trying to look down her blouse. They will have no idea of what jobs she has done or whom she's talked with, except for what she's said to them. Men and women think fundamentally differently and by encouraging women to demand a man who constantly shares his deepest thoughts, we're sending them down the wrong path because men rarely have deep thoughts and we're just setting women up to be continually disappointed.

Carl's Rephrase: I must have a partner who shares his feelings when appropriate and is honest with himself and me.

Emotionally Healthy...

I must have a partner who is emotionally healthy, and able to

share a stable life with someone else.

A good one and we all can agree with this one. Just one question for eHarmony - is there an insane person anywhere who doesn't think he's emotionally healthy? John Hinkley is convinced he's sane and that Jodi Foster will eventually share a stable life with him. Mark David Chapman believed that it was a perfectly sane and normal option to shoot John Lennon because he wouldn't give him an autograph. Everyone wants to be emotionally healthy and everyone assumes that they are. You might as well ask for somebody who breathes air.

Carl's Rephrase: I want someone who has a history of stable relationships and no history of arrests or hospitalization for mental illness.

Artistry...

I must have a partner who has a passion for music, literature, drama, art, and the finer things in life either as a spectator or participant.

Men are interested in drama, art, and music only as it helps them to get laid. Remember, Van Gogh cut off his ear to get a woman because his paintings weren't getting him anywhere. I have a friend who created an incredibly popular game that has been in use for years. Originally, it was created as a way for him and his friend to meet women at parties; it was just a fluke that turned it into a popular kid's game.

I also like the condescending sentence about the "finer things in life." As if baseball and sports are for the lower classes, while theatre and "literature" are for the special people. Those of us that don't like dramatic plays must not like "fine things." Very few men have a passion for drama and literature and most of those who do are gay.

Carl's Rephrase: I want a partner who will go with me to art museums and the theatre because he likes to share things with me.

Education...

I must have someone whose educational achievements match my own.

I wanted to check this one, mainly because I do enjoy hanging out with smart people. The problem is that education and smarts are generally pretty exclusive. Setting an arbitrary guideline of the same degree as you is an improper focus, especially if it concerns advanced degrees. People who desire and focus on educational achievements beyond a bachelor's degree are some of the dumbest and most boring people I've ever met. That's why they focus on educational achievements and it's how they compensate for their boring personalities driving away most of their friends.

For one six-month period when I was a member of eHarmony they kept matching me up with college professors and teachers with master's degrees. They were some of the most boring dates of my life. None of them offered an original thought or idea during any discussion. They were able to discuss the politics of their workplaces but none of them exhibited any characteristics of deep thought. Yet people I work with who don't have degrees are capable of far deeper and more intelligent conversations. In this world we focus on educational achievements as if they should be venerated and make people more qualified. In fact, it just shows that the person had enough money to go to school and enough brains to pass classes. That's not intelligence.

Not only is educational achievement overrated but the number one trait of stupid people is believing that they're smart. The main difference between smart people and stupid people is that smart people listen to other people. A stupid guy thinks he's smarter than everybody else, so he doesn't listen to anybody. He is the only expert worth considering. Smart people use lawyers when they're on trial, stupid people defend themselves.

Carl's Rephrase: I want someone whom I think is smart.

Patience...

I must have someone who can handle life's frustrations or momentary setbacks with a patient, steady demeanor.

Hell, if we could handle frustrations with a patient, steady demeanor we wouldn't have many frustrations or setbacks. That's why they're called frustrations; they frustrate and anger us. It's not healthy or normal to deal with them in a "patient, steady, demeanor." Humans aren't Vulcans; we have emotions (Bonus Star Trek reference for my fellow nerds). Not only that but women hate a man who doesn't get upset or mad every now and then.

Let's put this with the number one pick of all women from above; a man who is "sharing their deepest emotional thoughts and desires." Most women want both of these traits and can't understand that they're an oxymoron. Before you argue with me on this one, think of all your past relationships. How many times did you yell at the man, telling him that he needed to "be more expressive and say what you're feeling?" If we're stoic, we're "cold" and if we're emotional, we're "unable to handle things." This is why men die so much earlier than women.

Carl's Rephrase: I must have a partner who is able to cope with frustrations and momentary setbacks and doesn't let them stop him from leading a fulfilling life.

Tolerant...
I must have a partner who is able to hear and appreciate divergent viewpoints.

A good thought, but viewpoints on what? I mean, there's a world of difference between appreciating divergent viewpoints on the flat income tax versus seeing both sides in a discussion about lesbian porn (I'm for both, by the way). Once again, this presumes a black and white world. It assumes that there are open-minded and closed-minded people and nary the twain shall meet. Ridiculous.

Even worse, this is giving a license to kooks to go on being kooky. You know the person I mean – the one who isn't just a vegetarian, but also avoids honey because "bees are oppressed slaves working for human masters." This "must have" transfers the blame for a relationship not working from the kook to the normal person. After all, if you don't accept that the Mafia and J. Edgar Hoover conspired to kill JFK, then you're just unable to "appreciate divergent viewpoints." I think most people are open-minded, except when it comes to kooks.

Carl's Rephrase: I must have a partner who has the same kooky ideas as I do.

Attractiveness...

I must have a partner who is considered "very attractive" by most current standards.

We all know the people who check this one and we end up running into them more than we wish; the person who is so enamored with their own looks that they believe their mate must be as attractive as they believe they are. There are a thousand clichés about people who would check this requirement, but I must yield to Fred Sanford on this one. "Beauty is skin deep, but ugly goes right to the bone." Everybody wants someone who's attractive, but you cannot base a long-term relationship on appearance, much as we all would like to. A great short-term one, absolutely, but not a long-term one.

Let me digress for a minute about the incredibly unfair double standard that exists when it comes to men and women who insist on using looks as their main criteria for a partner. In every forum, women are constantly railing against guys who are interested in women for their looks, whether it's bashing a guy who looks at Playboy or a football fan ogling the cheerleaders. These guys are always portrayed as sexist louts, yet when women do the exact same thing, they're just "exercising taste."

Remember a few years ago when there was a Diet Coke ad that featured a handsome, muscular construction worker being admired by women? That ad was talked about by every group of women in every workplace. Nobody criticized those women for being shallow or sexist. In fact, women encouraged other women to talk about the ad and lust after the construction worker, who became a minor celebrity. Now fast forward to the release of the annual Sports Illustrated swimsuit issue. If a group of men talked about the cover model using the exact same words the women used, not only would they be called sexist and shallow, but at least one sexual harassment suit would be filed. Women admiring men for their looks is acceptable to women, but women will scorn men who admire women for their looks.

Carl's Rephrase: I must have someone who is "very attractive," which reveals just how shallow I am.

Personal Habits...
I must have a partner who maintains high standards of personal hygiene, orderliness, and other personal habits.

Hmmm, does any of us know anybody who doesn't maintain personal hygiene? I mean, who among us dates somebody that doesn't bathe? Actually, I do know some bohemians who don't bathe as often as the rest of us. However, those people believe that they have high standards of personal hygiene. Again, it's about self-knowledge and this option doesn't really define things properly. I believe that I'm relatively neat and clean, but I also know people who consider me a slob because I don't wash my sheets every week. If a person doesn't make the bed every morning or put every piece of clothing away in its proper place every time,

110

that's okay. It's the compulsive person whom this upsets who needs to readjust their attitude. As Roseanne Barr once said to a houseguest, "sorry the place is a mess, but we live here."

Carl's Rephrase: I must have someone who reminds me of Felix Unger.

Affectionate...

I must have someone who is comfortable giving and receiving affection.

Here's another qualification that fails to acknowledge the basic differences between men and women. It's not that we are uncomfortable giving and receiving affection; it's that we have a completely different definition of affection. Women seem to believe that giving and receiving affection requires flowers, candy, hand holding and little love notes in the mail. Men believe that handing someone a beer shows that we love them. Women who check this off still have an unrealistic portrait of how a man should behave and they're constantly disappointed when men don't meet their inaccurate fantasy.

It's not that we don't care, it's that we just don't think of things the same way that women do. It doesn't mean that we don't care if we don't remember to hold your hand every time we walk somewhere; it just doesn't occur to us that a one-month dating anniversary should be celebrated. It's okay to remind us - we don't mind. In fact, we'd rather know about it from you than have you mad at us for not remembering.

I know exactly what all of you women are saying; "You're missing the point. I want him to do things for me without being reminded of them." I want to win the lottery when I play it and that ain't happening either. Instead of constantly banging your head by having unrealistic expectations, why not remind him of something that you'd like? Let me give you two examples of interactions. First, the current one:

Man: (to woman who's been silent for the past hour) Something's wrong.

Woman: Yes.

Man: What?

Woman: You know.

Man: No, I don't.

Woman: Yes you do.

Man: No, I really don't.

Woman: What is today?

Man: Friday

Woman: And…

Man: Thank God It's Friday?

Woman: What happened one month ago today?

Man: We went to the Orioles game.

Woman: That's right, it was our first date.

Man: And?

Woman: And it was our first date exactly one month ago.

Man: Oh….happy anniversary!

The net result – one confused and angry man and one hurt and angry woman. Now, let's look at how the conversation should go when the woman takes into account the different ways of thinking between men and women.

Woman: (Listening to the radio) Boy, I love that Tori Amos.

Man: Me too.

Woman: I want to get her new CD, but I'm hoping somebody might get it for me as an anniversary present.

Man: (Still confused over what anniversary, but pretending to remember because he takes into account how differently men and women think) What an interesting dream. Maybe it'll come true.

The net result – a man who's reminded of an anniversary and given the perfect gift to buy making him relieved. He's also happy that the night might end with sex instead of a fight. Add to that a woman who's relieved because she's let her partner know

114

what's important to her and that happiness will also be increased on the actual anniversary when she receives a gift that she wants. Rather then getting upset at having to remind her partner of an anniversary, she's happy by realizing that he thought enough of her to celebrate it with her by giving her something that he knows she will enjoy.

Back to the original point, Carl's Rephrase: I must have someone who responds to my needs and wants **when** I express them.

Emotionally Generous...

I must have a partner who enjoys people and is generous with his or her compassion, attention, sympathies and love.

Carl's Rephrase: I want Dr. Phil.

Intellect...

I must have a partner who is bright and can share my understanding of the world as well as enjoy discussing important issues.

We're starting to get to into the good ones now. Once again, this falls victim to poor self-knowledge. Is there anybody who doesn't think they're bright? In fact, the stupider the person, the brighter they think they are. That's the major problem with stupid people – they think they're smart and so they refuse to listen to anybody else, thus aggravating every situation they encounter. And nobody likes sharing their view on important issues more than stupid people. If you don't believe me, just listen to any politician.

We all want someone who can share our understanding of the world, but what does that mean exactly? I can assure you that if I get ten people in a room, all of them will have a different understanding of the world and all of them will believe that their understanding is not just bright, but right, too. We all want someone who understands our world. What we need is help defining our world.

Carl's Rephrase: I must have a partner who is generally conservative politically and enjoys discussing important issues. (You can rewrite it also for liberal and middle of the road to match your particular philosophy.)

Unassuming...

I must have someone who is able to accept criticism, and even admit to being wrong sometimes.

Boy, is admitting you're wrong important to women. At least, it's important to them that we men admit that we're wrong. Guys, think of every relationship you've been in. Has it ever taken more than a month for the woman to tell you that you've done something wrong and then expect you to admit it? Never.

More importantly, what type of person admits right at the start that they're going to be offering criticism of their partner? Not only that, but that their partner should be ready to admit to being wrong? If you're opening up by saying that you're going to be criticizing, or you have had relationships fail because of your partner's inability to accept criticism, maybe it's your criticisms that are the problem! If this statement is important to you, you need to examine what you say and how you say it because I can guarantee you that your "criticism" is interpreted as irritating nagging, not helpful hints. By saying that your partner has to admit that you're right means that you have no leeway and no room to compromise in your discussions either. What a treat you must be.

I was on eHarmony and the woman I was matched up with had this listed as one of her Must Haves. Since I like to ask real questions, not the eHarmony generated questions, I asked the following question, "You mentioned that it's important to have a partner who accepts criticism and is able to admit being wrong. Can you give me an example of how you handled a situation where you admitted being wrong?" I thought it was a good, solid question that was based on her specific needs. Here's the response that I received:

While I recognize that it is important to be able to accept criticism, and I encounter this situation a lot as a manager dealing w/various types/ levels of individuals. Knowing that this doesn't really answer your question, I prefer not to be so specific at this stage.

Wow, that's an answer that would make a politician proud! Not a single grain of honesty or self-awareness in her answer. In fact, what she wanted from me was nothing that she was going to admit about herself.

Carl's Rephrase – I must have a partner who can accept me for the pain in the ass that I am.

Family Life...

I must have a partner who is committed to marriage, home, and family.

Carl's Rephrase – I must have a partner who loves the kids I already have and doesn't cheat like my previous partner.

Financial Responsible...

My partner must be financially responsible.

WARNING LIGHT!! I think most of us want someone who is financially responsible. I mean, at our age, you should have it together enough to have a job that doesn't involve supersizing food. People that check off this part of the form are showing that they, or their last partner, have some money issues. They want you to know that they're not prepared to date poor or overspending people. It's not a bad thing to want someone financially responsible, but if you have to mark it down, you're worrying about the wrong thing.

Carl's Rephrase: I want someone who shares financial decisions with me.

Sexually Abstinent...

I must have a spouse who has saved themselves sexually for marriage.

Carl's Rephrase: I want a fat guy.

Traditional...

I must have someone who is reserved and traditional in their sexual needs.

Carl's Rephrase: I must have a man who never asks for oral sex.

Sexually Knowledgeable...

I must have someone who is mature and experienced as a potential sexual partner and is able to express themselves freely.

All right, let's talk sex! Let's rephrase this for what it really says, "I want somebody who's good in bed." There's only one problem with this one. Who doesn't like to think of themselves as good in bed? There isn't a non-Jewish guy alive who's going to say he doesn't match this one. I have had women fall asleep during lovemaking, but I still consider myself good in bed.

I also had to laugh at the "mature and experienced" part of this one. As if maturity and experience have anything to do with good sex. Prostitutes are mature and experienced, but I sure as hell don't want to make love with one. Great sex depends on emotional intimacy and openness, not just the ability to stay hard for an hour. A guy would much rather have sex with an inexperienced and enthusiastic woman than an experienced woman who needs to be motivated.

Carl's Rephrase: I must have someone who is understanding and giving during sex, allowing for the greatest enjoyment possible for both partners.

Guideline #9

Breasts Aren't That Big a Deal

Or

DD is not Doubly Delicious

Sorry guys, this chapter is more for the female readers (although anything about breasts does fascinate men!). There are a ton of misconceptions out there about breasts and men's relationship with them. I thought I'd take this opportunity to clear up many of them.

First, and I realize that this isn't a surprise, men love breasts! The surprise may be that we love **ALL** kinds of breasts and there are all kinds out there for us. Small ones, big ones, pointy ones, lopsided ones, we love them all. There's virtually nothing about them we don't like, except that we don't get to see them enough.

What is a very difficult message for women to understand is that we do indeed love all sizes. I've been a man virtually my whole life and hung out with men a great deal and I can tell you with certainty that men love small breasts just as much as large breasts. In fact, we probably like them more. I would say that maybe ten percent of the guys I know have a large breast desire and there are as many guys who are turned off by huge breasts as there are guys in love with them. Yes, when we're in a pack of guys at a strip club and there's a huge-breasted woman on stage, we're all hooting and hollering and making comments. We may even watch a little big boob porn. However, porn and strip club behavior is not normal behavior nor does it reflect our actual attitudes. Our real life behavior is totally different from that. It's like the difference being at a football game versus work. At work we're not rooting for our opponent to be knocked out and have his leg broken but at a football game that's exactly what we want. It's a bit of aberrant behavior and shouldn't be used as a baseline for judging us, just as you shouldn't use behavior in a strip club as a baseline.

So why is there such a preoccupation with large breasts? It's a way for the cosmetic and fashion industry to become richer. Use special bras, have operations, use cream and you too can be popular. Generally not the case, but by the time you've found that out, they've got your money and they're not giving it back. In fact, if you talk with women who had large breasts in high school, you'll find that they wish they were smaller and that they dreaded the attention they received because of their breasts.

Yes, we do stare at big breasts, but that's because they're more obvious. Men love to look at breasts and we look at big breasts more because those are the ones we can see. Believe me, if every woman in the U.S. went topless for five years (one of the first steps a Birkmeyer Administration would implement), the impetus for large breasts would decrease dramatically. Big breasts are looked at because they're more obvious, not because we like them better than small breasts. We just like to see breasts! We'll

126

stare at small breasts in just a bra over large breasts in a loose sweater every time. The more we see, the better.

If you don't believe me, conduct an experiment. If you're an A or B cup, wear an outfit that reveals part of your breasts, but does not make them look larger. You will get twice as many looks because it's an opportunity for us to see some breast. We will **always** look at the person who has breasts that we can see in some way over the person whose breasts we can't see.

This brings me to the second point I'd like to make about breasts and that's for women to stop giving us a double message. Women will wear an outfit specifically designed and selected because it highlights their breasts. Then, when we respond by looking at them, we get in trouble! We're doing exactly what you asked us to do. When you picked out that outfit and that bra, you thought, "This'll show off my body to its best advantage," or something along those lines. You're right, it does and so we admire it by looking. Men are visual, you've selected a visual lure, and then you're upset when the outfit does precisely what you selected it to do? Why are we the culprit? If you don't want men to stare, then don't wear the outfit. I agree that you don't want to be treated as a piece of meat and I can see how it would get tiring and annoying after a while, but expecting men not to look at an obvious breast is like expecting the French to shower.

I've mentioned this to women and their response is pretty universal. They'll say that they want people to notice, but not stare and that they didn't give everybody a license to peek. That's the real problem - the lure you're using is not selective and you really want it to be selective. Even worse, you believe that it actually is selective. When a fisherman tosses a worm into the pond he knows it's going to be bitten by every fish that sees it. He's just hoping that one of the fish it attracts will be a nice bass or trout. When it's a sea robin, the fisherman doesn't blame the worm because he knows that the worm is attractive to all fish and there's no worm that only good fish will bite. It's the same with a nice bikini top. When you wear that top, you want Richard Gere to notice and whisk you away somewhere romantic. Unfortunately, there aren't a lot of Geres out there, and you're left with the rest of us being attracted. Since all men like breasts, all men are going to respond to an outfit that highlights them and it's ridiculous to think that it won't be that way. The guy you're interested in and the creep in the cubicle next door are going to examine the lure because we're all guys. The goal of a lure is to catch as many fish as possible. It's up to the person using the lure to pick and choose from the catch, not get mad at the fish that bite on the lure.

I know that Playboy and Penthouse have made it appear as if the only breasts that attract men are large ones. Let's look beyond those two magazines, read by a small minority of men, and take a look at general "sex symbols." Who are some of the top sex symbols of our time? Julia Roberts, Jennifer Lopez, Cindy Crawford, Elle MacPherson, Shannon Doherty, Sarah Michelle Geller, Jennifer Aniston, Britney Spears, Paris Hilton, Courtney Cox, Reese Witherspoon – not a chest bigger than a "C" cup among them. Is there a guy anywhere who doesn't lust after at least seven of those nine? Of course there isn't.

Let's look at Julia Roberts more closely (if we have to!). A solid "B" cup, she's made us drool in *Pretty Woman* and *Erin Brockavich*, along with being the sexiest Tinkerbell ever in *Hook*. The clothes she wears are revealing and sexy and she DOES NOT need huge breasts to accomplish that sexy look. Do we guys yearn to see more of her breasts? Absolutely. She's this generation's version of Farrah Fawcett, a woman who was lusted after by millions because of her breasts, yet they weren't big at all. They looked great and she showed you parts of them and that's what we really liked.

Now we'll look at Dolly Parton. She's famous for her enormous breasts but they're more of a joke to most people. Sure, guys would like to see her topless, but she's not considered a hugely sexual person, despite having huge breasts.

Take it even further. Name me a (non-porn star) sex symbol with breasts bigger than a "D" cup. Sophia Loren, Queen Latifah, Roseanne? That's about it and the reason for that is that the "B" is nice, "C" cup is ideal, "D" is fine, but anything bigger than that is for those guys with special tastes, not most guys.

Guideline #10

The Primary Motivation for Everything a Guy Does is

Sex

Or

We Really Can't Help It

Though you would think that women would have realized this around age twenty, it's something that never really seems to sink in – every decision a man makes is based upon sex in some way. It's a biological urge that is present in males and it dominates us completely. It does start to dim in the thirties and slowly fade, but it is always present and always a major force in our lives.

I know that a lot of you are dismissing this, saying you're well aware that men think with their penises a lot of the time. I'm telling you that it is **all** of the time and it is **all** of us. It's not just the obvious things like parachuting, surfing, and wearing clothes that we do for sex, it's everything. All of man's greatest achievements – the Hoover Dam, the pyramids, space travel - were done by guys who thought it would help them get laid. It's why I'm writing this book.

The testosterone in our bodies gives us a tremendous amount of energy and when that energy is not being released sexually, it will still come out somehow. The reason why men watch and cheer and are obsessed with sports is to take away some of that energy. When our team wins, that energy increases, and we want sex more than ever. That's why men riot after their team wins the Super Bowl – we can't get laid and we have to release that energy somehow. When our team loses, we still want sex, but we lose the energy to find a woman so we just beat off.

It's also why men are so good at waging war. From the moment puberty hits, our goal is to have sex, or failing that, to see women with as little clothes on as possible. When you're an adolescent, you develop elaborate plans to enable you to spend more time with women and to see women naked. It can be changing the route you walk to school so that you can walk near somebody you like, arranging your college class schedule or even picking a career. Hell, if a law were passed today banning women from dating musicians, there wouldn't be a group still playing tomorrow.

Let me give you an example from college. My good friend Ken briefly met this girl named Lisa at a school event and he decided that he wanted to go out with her. Since everybody at school had to eat dinner in the cafeteria (long story), Ken started looking for her at dinner. After spending two hours a day in the cafeteria for a week or so, we discovered that Lisa usually ate around 6:10 and she usually went to the right tray line to get her food and then went left to get a Coke. We decided that the best place for Ken to make contact would be at the Coke machine, so we devised a plan where we'd be talking nearby and when Lisa was 20 feet away from the Coke machine, Ken would head over there and then he could offer to pour her soda. After four days of waiting, our timing was correct and Ken was able to casually approach her and begin a conversation. They dated for about six months, with Lisa always telling the story of how they "accidentally bumped into each other at the Coke machine," not realizing that two weeks of planning and scheming went into that accidental meeting. As we grow older, that planning skill transfers over to war, which is why the Normandy invasion was successful.

The origins of that intense sex drive are pretty simple. When the human race began, the ultimate goal bred in us was survival. The best way to ensure survival of the race is to produce as many offspring as possible. So God gave men a strong sex drive that overcomes everything else because that would let the human race survive. Conversely, since pregnancy used to be a very dangerous medical condition, women were genetically designed to not reproduce frequently. They don't desire sex as much after having a child because the female body needs time to recover and regain strength. Now, the urges to survive and reproduce are still a part of our DNA and no matter how enlightened the man pretends to be, he is still driven by the same urges that allowed his ancestors to survive. The intense sexual drive of men is normal and genetically based. If men are expected to accept the emotional changes brought on to a woman by the biology of her period, then women must accept the biologically driven sexual drive of men.

It's really not even that bad once you understand and accept it. However, too many women refuse to accept it and instead try to change it. Using that lovely double standard again, men are expected to alter their biologically driven needs, yet understand the biologically driven mood swings of PMS. I'm not saying that women must give in to a man's every sexual need and desire, just understand that it is a normal and natural biological function for us. Understand it by realizing that it's behind everything we do. And, if you make fun of it, then prepare to have your mood swings mocked as well.

Let me give a few examples of how men's brains work automatically. When we first see a woman, we immediately size her up sexually. If she is acceptable to us, and this ranges widely from guy to guy, then every decision we make is based on that aspect and will be part of a sometimes conscious and sometimes subconscious desire to have sex with her. If we don't want to have sex with her, then all of our decisions about her are based on the fact that we don't need or want her approval.

Take a look at your local McDonalds. If there are two women working the cash register, we'll always go to the prettier one. It's not even a conscious decision; it's just what we do. If there's a problem with the order, we'll accept it with a smile from the pretty one. If the problem order is delivered by an unattractive person, then we'll complain or give them a hard time. The thought "if I'm nice she'll have sex with me," isn't a conscious thought, but our instincts take over. We aren't thinking "I could get laid next to the fry machine and pick up some fries at the same time," but an unconscious part of us makes us be nice in case that were to ever happen.

This guideline actually has a very powerful message for women, if they understand and accept it. That incredibly strong male urge for sex means that women have all of the power in a relationship. Women should use that power to ensure that they get everything they want sexually. There are a ton of books, radio shows, and magazine articles that talk about how men don't always please women sexually. If a guy doesn't do what you need to enjoy yourself, then speak up. Tell him what you need or you'll cut him off. A relationship is about reciprocity and if you are providing something that the man needs, then the man needs to do the same for you. Use that power we gave you. Though you shouldn't use sex as a weapon, it can be used as a bribe, as long as that doesn't become the sole reason for having sex. If you use it every now and then to get us to clean the basement, we won't mind.

Guideline #11

Men Don't Like to Talk

Or

Quiet, the Game's On!

This is a huge complaint with women – men don't talk about their feelings often enough. Yet when we do talk about our feelings, we get in trouble. "What do you feel about this?" is a question we're always asked. When we answer truthfully, "I don't care," then we get in trouble. The fact is that we, as men, don't care about a lot of things and when we do care about something; we do not need to discuss it. Even worse, when we do show our sensitive side, it's often a big turn-off for women, despite their lectures to the contrary. If we appear vulnerable or even cry we'll be mocked for not being strong enough. There's something in a woman's DNA that makes her not like a sensitive man as a lover.

In one of the early phases used by the eHarmony dating service, there's a list of forty-plus multiple-choice questions. You are supposed to pick five from the list and send them to your potential date to be answered. Every single woman that I've corresponded with has sent at least one question that involves my discussing my feelings. Mind you, this is in our initial contact – the very first thing they want to know about is how much I discuss my feelings. Here's the question asked most often:

What of the following scares you the most?

A. Giving a speech before 500 people.

B. Going on a long car ride with someone I just met.

C. Sharing my deepest fears with my partner.

D. A meeting with the president of my corporation.

Now, despite the best efforts of eHarmony and women to disguise the intent of this question, it's quite clear that the entire purpose is to confirm that men will answer "C," or to answer something other than "C" to show we like to share our deepest fears. It's what women expect, that we're afraid to show our feelings, but that's not the correct answer. The plain truth is that we don't need to express our feelings all of the time because we know our feelings and they're not that deep or significant. We don't talk about them because we accept them and deal with them subconsciously and we don't understand why women don't understand that and need to constantly talk about it. Here's how that question should read:

What of the following scares you the most?

A. Having to watch the Yankees win another World Series.

B. Going on a car ride in a Yugo that doesn't have a radio.

C. Hearing "we need to talk" from your partner.

D. The cable TV going out.

Here's another example, taken from the greatest guy movie of all time, *Lethal Weapon 2*. I know that just that movie title bothers women, as it's a sequel and it has the word "weapon" in it, but it's the perfect movie to watch if you want to understand men. Danny Glover and Mel Gibson are partners and best friends in it. In one scene, Glover is trapped by a bomb and Gibson risks his life to stay with him and help him survive the blast. Right before they try to escape the bomb, the following conversation takes place:

> Glover: Riggs, I just want to say.....you know.
>
> Gibson: Yeah, I know.
>
> Glover: I really mean it.
>
> Gibson: I know you do.

See, no sappy definitions or descriptions are needed. They know exactly how each other feels because they're there. They're present in the moment with each other, not seeking alternate meanings and explanations. Their every action shows the deep bond they have and trying to put it in words is completely inadequate. Words lie; actions don't, so men use actions to show

how they feel. A pat on the ass, a thump on the arm, a nod, those are all we need. Men don't often discuss deep thoughts because, except for some dead Greek philosophers, we really don't have any. If you want to know a man's true feelings and character, examine his behavior. It's easy to talk a good game, much harder to live a good life.

Men accept things and we do not analyze them or the behaviors behind them. We don't analyze our relationships with other guys and we certainly don't seek to place roles on our girlfriends and ourselves. Why do you think all of those books that identify personality types are written for and read by women? There's no male equivalent of Dr. Phil because we don't think in that manner. There is no book, "Men Who Love Too Much." It's not because we don't love too much, it's because we don't think about it or analyze it. We "do."

We're creatures of action and instinct and that's how we judge the world, though it's not a conscious process. Men also assume that everyone is like us and since we don't need to "talk about" things, we don't realize that women need to talk about things.

None of that chit chat that women seem to crave is necessary in male-to-male interaction. That's why when women demand it; we find ourselves inexperienced at participating in it and puzzled by the request. We don't think in that way and rather than women blaming men for "not being able" to verbalize our emotions, how about blaming women for needing men to verbalize? You're expecting us to behave in a way that's foreign to our inherent nature and it will result in nothing but frustration for both of us. It's another double standard and it's wrong. Let me flip it around to illustrate.

Men want and need sex for a satisfying relationship. Yet, it's "wrong" for us to demand sex from our wives and steady partners. Hell, we can even be arrested for it. It's something that's not too difficult and yet every single guy I know has had their partner turn them down for sex on multiple occasions. We're then made to feel bad just for asking, even though it's incredibly important to us and to our feelings about the relationship. It's not that hard for women to have sex, so why not just do it to please us?

I'm sure most women reading those paragraphs are now outraged. Let me be clear – I'm not advocating forcing a woman to have sex. I am advocating that in order to please their partners women should sometimes have sex when they don't feel like it. There is no difference between men needing sex and women needing verbal affirmations. Each partner sometimes has to do something that they don't feel like doing or makes them slightly uncomfortable to please the other. Why is it okay for women to not have sex and it's wrong for men to not discuss their feelings?

The answer is actually simple – our need for sex outweighs our unwillingness to express ourselves and so we do one to get the other. Men have realized that refusing to discuss our "feelings" means a pissed-off woman and a pissed-off woman is never going to have sex. So for decades we've given the okay to this double standard because we're too weak to go without sex and really force the issue.

Guideline #12

Actions Are What Matters

Or

Don't Listen to Me

"I know he's not that nice to my parents, but he's great to me."

"I always have to arrange things and be the one who calls, but he really loves me and I love him."

"That time he was arrested was not his fault. He was with some friends who were having a loud party and the cop was a jerk and just decided to arrest everybody."

Do any of the above phrases sound familiar? Are you constantly making excuses to your friends and family for your boyfriend or girlfriend's behavior? More importantly, are you making excuses for yourself?

The plain truth is that in relationships, as in life, actions are what matter because they are the true barometers of a person. It's easy to say things that we don't mean to get what we want, but it's a lot harder to do the things that are necessary to get what we want. That's why you should not remain in a relationship where the words do not match the actions of your partner.

Let's look at the example of my friend Bonnie. Bonnie is 38, works in sales, and has two boys under the age of ten. Her husband Paul is a salesman and really appears to be a nice guy. Always friendly and eager to help, you'd think he'd be an ideal husband. In fact, he constantly tells Bonnie that he loves her and the boys.

Every day when he comes home from work, the first thing that Paul does is examine the house to make sure that it's clean and everything is in its proper place, a determination that only he can make. After Bonnie serves him his meal, Paul goes into their basement and watches TV until it's time for bed. Three nights a week, he goes to the gym and works out after dinner and then heads straight for the basement as soon as he gets home. Bonnie's reaction, "I know it doesn't seem like it, but he really does love me and the boys."

He probably does, but it doesn't matter because he does not behave as a person who loves his family should behave. A relationship must be mutual and every one of Paul's reactions shout out that his needs are all that matter. He doesn't help with the cooking, cleaning, or raising of the boys. An occasional night playing and a few weekend activities are not enough to make Paul a good father or partner. If you love another person, you must behave that way and that often includes some element of self-sacrifice. People unwilling to sacrifice (and I mean emotionally, not physically) are not capable of true intimacy and without true intimacy, a loving relationship is impossible. You don't have to give up nights with the boys or girls and a good partner will even encourage that. It's when those independent times negatively impact the time and effort you put into your relationship that you have crossed the line between independence and selfishness.

Another acquaintance of mine illustrates the point further. Lynn was 28 and divorced when she met Juan, a construction worker and apparently nice guy. One initial awkward moment occurred when Lynn found out that Juan had a criminal record.

Juan's story was plausible. He was with some friends having a bachelor party at a strip club when one member of the group jumped on the stage. The bouncers "overreacted" and tried to throw them out. They resisted and fought with the bouncers "because we hadn't done anything wrong," and the cops came and arrested Juan and one of his friends. They hadn't really done anything wrong, but "the cops were real jerks and had to arrest somebody and they picked on Juan because he mouthed off to them."

Plausible. Stupid, but plausible. The problem is that it's not true and it does illustrate that Juan has a violent side, as we did unfortunately find out later. Whenever you hear a story about how a person has been "wronged by the Man," you need to examine the story with a microscope because it's almost always the storyteller's fault, not the fault of "the Man." Most courts use the guideline: What would a reasonable person do in this situation?" Let's apply that to Juan's story.

First, a reasonable person doesn't jump up on stage with a stripper. Everyone that walks into a strip club knows that to get on stage or harass the girls immediately invites trouble. If you decide that doing that is reasonable, when the bouncer tells you to stop and get off the stage, a reasonable person does just that. He doesn't start arguing and fighting with the bouncer. And when the police are called, a reasonable person does not start arguing with the police, he immediately becomes polite. Juan's behavior clearly was over the line and wrong in this example, yet his words convinced Lynn that his actions were not important. She continued seeing him for several months, until he hit a friend of hers, causing a fight that was far more painful emotionally than physically. All that mess could have been avoided if she had just followed guideline twelve.

Now I'm sure that some of you are saying, "that's pretty harsh, a lot of people do dumb things and that doesn't make them bad people." You're right. However, Juan had not accepted that he had done anything wrong to get arrested. The initial fight was the bouncer's fault and the arrest was the cops' fault. Nothing was Juan's fault, he just happened to be there and get arrested. His actions – a criminal arrest – did not match his explanation – I was an innocent bystander. When that happens, it's the actions that matter, not the words. Unfortunately, most people follow the reverse. I remember listening to a female friend describe a boyfriend's incarceration for armed robbery as him "just asking a guy on the street for money and he happened to have a gun and the cops called it armed robbery." Stupid behavior and criminal behavior can be accepted if they're not habitual and if the person believes and states those behaviors are wrong.

In today's world we have an unfortunate tendency to excuse or explain away criminal behavior and/or incarceration. Illegal immigrants are now "undocumented aliens." Tax cheats are now "wily businesspeople." When they get caught, it's never their fault and no one seems to be outraged. Heck, we tend to blame the agency that arrests them for persecuting them. I know someone that didn't pay any taxes for three years and when the IRS came after him and he was forced to sell his business to pay back taxes and penalties, it was the "damn IRS' fault" and they cost him his business. His family and friends all agree with him. Nobody mentions how he consistently broke the law over a period of years that caused the IRS to come after him. Nobody mentions how if he had followed the law he wouldn't have had to sell his business but he might not have been able to afford that trip to Vegas. His behavior, and that of too many other lawbreakers, is ignored and it's the fault of "the Man."

The real question you have to ask yourself is - are you constantly making excuses for him? If you have to constantly explain his behavior to others, then he's a bad guy and the only person you're convincing with your excuses is you.

Guideline #13

Less History, More Mystery

Or

Shut Up Already!

A simple guideline, but oh how difficult! Since we're all in the scratch and dent section, we all obviously have some scratches. Some of them are hidden, and some are right out in the open. What nobody wants is to hear a history of how you got every one of your scratches. Telling us the history magnifies the scratches.

We expect scratches. Heck, we've got a few ourselves, but listening in detail to every wrong that has been done to you is not only boring, it's irritating. We don't care. The fact that Bob stood you up ten years ago and how it should have been a warning sign but you just ignored it and kept going out with him and he kept treating you that way so now you're distrustful of everybody is just way too much.

I don't want to hear what made you the person you are today – I want to get to know that person. Then, once I know you, I'd like to learn more details about your life and history. It must be spaced out however, not all crammed into the first date.

One of my first post-divorce dates was a bitter thing named Trudy. A friend of mine (we're not speaking anymore) suggested I call her and I did. In the first five minutes of our first date, she wanted to know all about my marriage, my divorce, and how many long-term relationships I had had. She then proceeded to go into detail about all of her past relationships. That's relationships, with an "s."

Trudy wasn't the only one. I would say that a solid thirty percent of the women I dated insist on saying something derogatory about the ex-husband on the first date. For women with kids, it's almost a given. I was e-mailing Jessica to get to know her before we met and in one of the first e-mails she told me about her son and her ex-husband:

> *I think this is in contrast to the fact that his father does so much with him that is over the top on the weekends that he has him, that I try to show Michael that you don't have to spend a lot of money on someone to have a good time. The worse thing that I think I could do for Michael is to try and play the game of buying his love like his jerk of a father does. I know that my son loves me and he knows that I love him dearly. One of these days, Michael will see his father for what and who he is.*

I agree with her in that the worst thing that she can do is play the game of buying his love. I actually applaud her efforts to teach her son that the important things in life don't need to be expensive. However, I don't want to hear about how awful his

155

father is, even if it's a veiled reference. In fact, the veiled anger and disgust at the father is worse than saying "he was a cheater." I know that complaining about exes is a popular sport and it's really popular among women as they bond in the Sisterhood of the Bitter Divorcées and Separatees (also known as SOBS). The problem is that the more you complain about your ex, the worse a person you make him out to be and the worse it reflects on YOU. You married a guy that was a horrible person. In fact, you not only decided that this horrible person was someone that you wanted to spend the rest of your life with, but you then decided that this awful human being was somebody that should be the father of your children. The more you tell me how bad he is, the more I wonder just how skewed is your compass?

Now, we have all misread people and we have even gotten into relationships with bad or hurtful people. We also have been in relationships with people who changed at some point. However, taking the next step and marrying them, then starting a family with them, is a bigger step. You can say it's not your fault that you

156

married a person who turned bad, but chances are there were a lot of signs he was bad that you missed. In fact, I'll bet that if you ask your friends they'll tell you they had issues with him. Still, being with a bad person happens, especially to people who marry at a young age. But yes, no matter what happened in your relationship, part of it is your fault. That's okay though. We all make mistakes. We all need to take responsibility and realize that a marriage doesn't feature one horrible person and one angel. Something happens with both of you and a lot of times the horrible person is fed and encouraged by their mate. So the more you complain about how horrible he/she is, the more I wonder how big a part you played in that.

A friend of mine is married to someone she doesn't like that much. One of her big complaints is that they get in big fights over him being "messy." If he makes dinner, he doesn't clean the kitchen to her satisfaction and he'll "leave the kitchen in shambles." So she makes every meal and cleans every room in the house. After all, if she left it to him, he's so awful that "he'll destroy it or not clean it up that night." When he does that, she gets mad and they get into a huge fight. In fact, it happens regularly.

I suggested that she stop playing the game. Ask him to clean up the kitchen after she cooks and if he doesn't do it right away, don't clean it for him. If he starts to yell or argue, tell him that you're not going to do that and go into another room. Or go for a walk. Don't play the game and dance the dance of chaos. Take a deep breath and be calm and he will be unable to be the angry jerk because you're not feeding that fire. If he does, or if it escalates to where you're feeling scared, then immediately get out and get professional help. But before that step, if you don't create the scene, it can't usually happen.

She refuses to do that because she has a need for everything to be clean. That's fine, it's her decision. However, every time she complains about her husband being horribly messy and a jerk, I know that there's a second side to that story and that she's stoking his fire somewhat. When women complain about their exes early in a relationship, it's a warning sign all right, but one that warns us away from you, not him.

There is one thing worse than complaining about exes or discussing other unsavory aspects of your life to this point. That's the woman who starts discussing her sexual history. Now, men normally like to hear a woman talk about sex because it makes it more likely that we're going to have sex with her. We're already thinking about sex with her, so a tiny picture or two sometimes helps. What we don't need to hear are details or bizarre stories. Let me get to know you before I find out that you like Crisco Oil and rubber sheets. Bringing it up on an early date just means that we think of you as a little kooky. Bringing it up after we've established a relationship means that we think that whatever you like might be fun to try and how about now?

The worst variation of this is, hands down, the woman who tells the story about how she used to be unbelievably wild sexually. Sometimes it's with one guy and sometimes it lasted for a couple of years, but it was a time of her life filled with wild sexual

159

adventures, a ton of desire, and an aggressive need for sex. Our first thought is "great!" but that hope is immediately dashed when the woman then tells us how she's not that way anymore and never wants to be that way again. It's like telling a Little Leaguer that he's made the major leagues and then he never actually plays in a game. You're telling us that you had that sexual relationship of which every guy dreams about, but that it's never going to happen again. None of us wants the conservative woman. We want the woman you just described to us. Even if we only have her for a weekend. Please don't tell us that there was a great show but it's closed and will never return.

Guideline #14

People Who Do Nutty Things Are Nutty

Or

The Spaghetti Personality Theory

Many times in today's society we see somebody commit a horrible crime and the response from family members and friends is the same: "He just snapped. Before hacking up his family and putting them in little plastic bags, he was a perfectly normal guy." Absolutely no way is that possible. Bad behavior does not magically appear and bad behavior in one aspect of a person's life indicates that **he is a bad person**, not that he just happens to have a slight personality flaw.

Let's start in serious mode and then work our way down. One of the earliest indicators of psychopathic personalities is that during childhood they injure and often torture animals. That specific behavior indicates a greater disturbance and the way that these mentally ill individuals grow sicker is by having that behavior ignored. Disturbed behavior is a symptom of a disturbed mind and is not to be ignored.

Now when we're discussing dating, it's not as clear-cut as psychopathic behavior, but the same general principles hold. We like to pretend that a person's mind is like a battleship, with hundreds of airtight compartments that can easily be sealed off from one another. That way, if a bomb explodes in one compartment of the battleship, that section is shut down and cut off from the rest of the ship. The problem is contained and the overall ship is fine and able to continue sailing. That's how many people want to believe a mind works. A person that steals from work just has one bad compartment and isn't entirely bad. We don't have to toss out the ship because of that one bad compartment. It's nice to believe, but it's completely untrue.

Our minds are more like plates of spaghetti, with all of the strands weaving together to form the whole dish. One strand touches most other strands and it's impossible to remove one strand without impacting most of the other strands. In fact, one really bad strand of spaghetti will really permeate the entire dish and render it inedible.

The way our society thinks, a person who treats his parents badly and his girlfriend well is an okay person who just "has issues with his parents." We think he's a battleship, with his parent compartment sealed off. Unfortunately, a person who treats his parents badly will not be able to contain that behavior and it will eventually spill over into his relationship with his girlfriend because behavior overlaps, it's not separate.

Let me try to give you a good dating example. I know somebody who spends a great deal of time studying the assassination of John F. Kennedy, looking for clues to the conspiracy behind his death. It may seem like a harmless hobby, but it indicates a person who is not able to see things properly. A person who sees conspiracy in that will also see conspiracy in other aspects of his life and be suspicious in general.

Let's follow that example by looking at Oliver Stone. JFK is an excellent film, but it's fiction in which inconsistencies and facts are overlooked in order to prove his point. It's a very personal film, obviously reflecting his beliefs. Stone sees conspiracy because he wants to see it and that mindset permeates all of his films. Look at his films or read any interview with Stone and you can clearly see that suspicious, paranoid mindset. JFK is not a separate strand of his life, it's part of his life, and by looking at the one we get insight into the other.

How many of you would be willing to date someone who wrote this in their dating profile?

I live a healthy life and don't follow the doctors who just want to market a bunch of pills to you. Depression, anxiety, high blood pressure, and cholesterol don't need drugs you can just change what you eat and make them all go away but corporate doctors don't want you to know that.

Don't fall for their lies. So don't contact me if you

are taking any medication. I'm drug free and proud

of it!

I plucked that out of someone who contacted me on

Plentyoffish.com. We won't even get into the idea that many

medications are necessary or argue health care. Does anyone really

want to get into a conversation with this person?

How about a more harmless example? Let's examine those

people who are greatly into Renaissance Fairs. I'm sure you have

them in your location – events that celebrate life in the Middle

Ages with food, costumes, and re-creations of life in that time

period. A mildly enjoyable way for nerds to spend a day, there's

nothing wrong with a Renaissance Fair in and of itself.

But, a person who attends every day or wears an elaborate

costume to the fair is a person with a personality flaw. It's not a

serious one, but there's something there if a person is so enamored

of another time and place that their yearly highlight is dressing as a jester and drinking mead. It's telling you that they're severely unhappy or out of place in their current life and are seeking to escape. That's why people like that hang out together; they feed on each other's neuroses.

You can substitute Star Trek conventions for Renaissance Fairs and you've got basically the same situation. There's nothing wrong with enjoying Star Trek and if you want to meet William Shatner, go right ahead. If you can recite every episode from memory, have a completely authentic Starfleet captain's uniform, speak Klingon, or have every episode memorized, there's a problem. You're avoiding real life by entering a fantasy world.

I believe that a great deal of our society's problems today got their start in the Sixties, when the concepts of right and wrong became ridiculed. Instead of stating that certain behaviors were wrong, we tried to "understand" the reasons behind those behaviors. That's okay, but we took it too far and decided that the behavior wasn't as important as the reasons for that behavior. The reasons are now the excuse for the behavior and that excuse is used to suddenly cast the person committing the crime in a positive light.

You see this when you read about a criminal being sentenced. The defense attorney argues for a short sentence because the convicted criminal had a rough childhood or was poor or is a drug addict. All too many times the judges buy that bullshit and give the criminal a lighter sentence. In Maryland, we had a disgusting criminal who beat a 24 year-old Burger King Manager to death because he recognized the robber as a former employee. Rightfully, the murderer was given the death penalty. That was overturned by the Court of Appeals because the jury didn't give enough weight "to his abusive childhood." Why a person murders is unimportant because murder is wrong. Period. It violates one of the basic precepts of a civilized society and it can not be excused because of childhood trauma. Explained, yes, but not excused.

What does that rant have to do with dating? Simple; there are fundamental precepts in dating and people who violate those precepts are not good people and should not be dated, nor should excuses be made for them. The basic precepts:

1. Treat your partner with honesty and respect.

2. Treat their family and friends with respect.

3. Work to provide for their basic physical and emotional needs.

4. Work to keep them free from fear and danger.

That's it. Pretty simple rules, aren't they? Yet millions of people violate these rules daily and their partners accept it. Even worse, they'll make excuses for it and their resulting unhappiness!

My friend Michelle is a perfect example of this syndrome. She was dating a guy named Brian who was a complete jerk. He was good looking, I'll say that, and he could be fun at times. However, he just plain treated people badly, especially service workers. If there was a mistake with a meal he ordered, he wouldn't calmly ask for it to be fixed, he'd berate the poor waiter or waitress and let that anger control him for the rest of the night.

Though never violent, his bursts of anger against people who "wronged" him were considerable and frightening.

Michelle used to brush them off, saying that "he had a tough childhood. His father was really rough on him to be perfect and he's hard on everybody because of it. Besides, he is never that way with me." Well, as anyone who didn't have a crush on him would realize, Brian eventually did turn that anger on her with a blistering verbal attack that had Michelle in tears for a week. Even then she wouldn't dump him because "I love him." Love involves following my precepts of respect and anyone who consistently violates those rules does not deserve your love. Finally, as Brian's anger turned on Michelle more and more, she dumped him. However, he put her through two months of hell before she found the strength to let her sense of self overcome her "love" for him. Those months wouldn't have been miserable for her if she had followed my guideline and realized that bad behavior means you're a bad person.

Guideline #15

There's No Such Thing as a Good Fix-Up

Or

I Don't Care That You Know a Great Person For Me

There are many things that we can learn from watching television and not all of them have to do with making your dishes brighter. A common comedy plot is when the married couple in the sit-com decides to fix-up a single friend of the husband or wife with another single friend, or relative, or postman. You've seen it a hundred times, the wife wants to fix up the husband's co-worker with Cousin Sue and despite her husband's objections she does it anyway. Of course, the match is terrible and the sit-com audience is left in stitches. Real life is basically the same, except there's no audience to be entertained and the hurt feelings are real.

I have adopted an unusual strategy for fix-ups. I just go on them. It's a hundred times easier to go on one bad date than have to spend days explaining why you know it's going to be a bad date. You see, the people attempting the fix-up are well-meaning, convinced that they're doing the right thing and that they know what's best for you. By challenging the fix-up, they believe that you're challenging their taste. You are challenging their taste, but it's not an insult, it's just that people are different.

I understand the concept behind the fix-up. When I was married I thought about it myself. You want everybody to be as happy as you are, so you try to match people up in your head. If you like Bob and Betty, why wouldn't Bob and Betty like each other? Heck, let's call them today! A noble thought, and even an understandable one, but fix-ups are about as successful as the Buffalo Bills were in the Super Bowl.

It's important to distinguish between the two types of fix-ups. There's the traditional fix-up, when somebody who knows you well wants to fix you up with somebody else that they know well. In that circumstance, the Fixer is actually taking into account the various personality traits of the Fixees and considers whether or not a fix-up would actually work.

Then, there's the Mrs. Paul's Fix-Up. The Fixer decides that she (it's usually women that want to create a fix-up) wants to fix up a certain person, but isn't sure who to fix them up with. So, like a fisherman working for Mrs. Paul's, she casts a wide net into her ocean of friends and acquaintances, hoping to find something useful in there. Those who are fortunate enough to be married or engaged are able to wiggle out of the net, but everybody else is tossed into it and dumped on board.

The Mrs. Paul's Fix-Up usually goes like this – "hey, my friend Carl is single and not dating anybody, but he should be, so whom can I fix him up with?" Then, they go through their list of friends and, if they're single, they're perfect! Here's some of the lines I've been told by people attempting a Mrs. Paul's Fix-Up:

> She liked the Spiderman movie and you used to read comic books as a kid, so you two have a lot in common.

You have a great sense of humor and she likes to laugh.

I know you're a good cook and she loves to eat, so what could be a better match?

Just an aside – there is virtually nothing worse to say about a prospective date than "she loves to eat." Even Gandhi would run screaming from that fix-up.

The sure sign of a Mrs. Paul's Fix-Up is a person who tries to fix you up multiple times. One friend of mine tried a second fix-up before the end of the first fix-up date! Perhaps she felt guilty because the first girl she fixed me up with left before dessert, but that's a story for another chapter. A person attempting to fix you up multiple times is not considering your personality or your needs, she just wants you paired up.

This is where the real insidious nature of all fix-ups comes into play. You see, since their motives are noble, Fixers assume that you will be grateful. Not just grateful, but they will actually get upset with you if you do not get involved with the person. Yes, in order to maintain the friendship, you have to date the person several times. No matter that you find her as appealing as a plate of raw liver, the only feelings that seem to count are those of the Fixer. I'm not sure why this occurs with relationships and nothing else, but it does. If a friend likes to cook and asks you to try a new recipe, she doesn't yell at you if you don't like the dish. Yet if the same person fixes you up and you don't like their choice for you, suddenly you're an uncooperative jerk. Why is that?

Let me give you an example of this entire process. My friends Tracy and Paul have tried several times to fix me up, with all of them being disastrous. The latest attempt was the best, sad as that may be.

Yep, it began with that dreaded phrase, "I have a friend at work who's nice and funny…" At that point, everything Tracy said was as if it were being uttered by Charlie Brown's teacher, as my mind instantly began to race for reasons to get out of what I knew was coming up.

"She used to be a chef and I know how much you love to cook," enthused Tracy, "so I thought you guys might really hit it off." A long description then was given, much of it as useful as a used car salesman's spiel. I've taken up the tactic of just listening and not asking questions, as no answer you receive at this stage will give you useful information.

"So I thought we could all go out for dinner one night," Tracy went on, oblivious to my discomfort. "It wouldn't be a fix-up or date or anything like that. It would be me and Paul, Susan from work and her husband Steve, my friend Marcia and you." Foolish me. Why in the world would I think that two married couples and one single couple would be anything at all like a group date?

I told Tracy that I wasn't really interested, looking to Paul for some support. Unfortunately, though we guys have an unstated agreement to help each other out, it's obliterated by the guy's realization that no sex will be forthcoming for him if he comes out against this idea. Tracy's mission was not to be deterred by my lack of interest; it just spurred her on more.

Like most guys, I'm not big for getting into emotional talks. At the time, I didn't have a list of reasons why I didn't want to get fixed up again and bringing up the previous bad attempts just makes women madder. You see, they actually believe that the reason the fix-up went wrong is not their choice of dates, but your stupidity. Other than saying, "Your taste sucks," I had no retort that would stop the fix-up train, so I finally agreed.

We would all meet for dinner the next week and I would meet Marcia, the 14th girl who would be perfect for me. Alas, perfection is still beyond my grasp.

I got to the dinner about five minutes late, which isn't too bad, especially given traffic near the restaurant. Tracy and Paul were there, as was the other couple, but Marcia hadn't arrived yet. I had a seat and joined in the conversation, but since it was about people at their work that I didn't know, I really couldn't contribute much.

Marcia arrived about five minutes later. She was cute, but with a strong element of toughness clearly present on her face. This was somebody who had had a hard life. Marcia was seated across from me and we exchanged pleasantries, but the conversation quickly moved on to a group conversation. Again, since they all were friends and four of them worked at the same place, there wasn't a lot that I could contribute to the conversation.

That changed about five minutes after Marcia's arrival when the subject switched over to politics. A very dangerous topic at any time, but especially during a get acquainted meal. Now, as you may have guessed, politically I'm a conservative, but I have some very liberal leanings on some subjects. Whenever I'm in a group setting like this, however, I try to be neutral, as politics is just an inflammatory subject.

Unfortunately, this group hadn't heard of this policy and they went off attacking a Republican elected official. It wasn't a slight disagreement either; it was a vicious personal attack, the kind that makes you squirm even when you agree with the

177

sentiments. It was a Glenn Beck type of attack. I didn't participate or argue because you can't win in these arguments, so I just let people express themselves.

I would say that this subject went on for about ten minutes, when Marcia said, "we haven't asked Carl how he feels. You're not a Republican are you?"

"Yep, I am," I replied. "I have a mixed bag of policies, but I lean more towards the Republican side in a lot of arguments." That's all I said. I didn't attack their position or their candidates; I just calmly stated that I was a Republican. Well, as far as the table was concerned, I had just come out in favor of puppy killing. There was an awkward silence for a minute and then Tracy changed the subject.

Needless to say, the rest of the night didn't go so great. It didn't go poorly, but it was clear that Marcia and I were completely different people. The conversations went well, but it was very difficult for me to get into a lot of the discussions because I didn't know any of the people who were brought up and the political discussion made it clear we should stay away from national topics. The few times I brought up topics to Marcia, they weren't good topics for her and the conversation didn't flow. I don't remember her making any attempt to involve me in a conversation.

The dinner ended and we all went home. It wasn't an awful date, except for the political part, but it wasn't great either. Marcia and I were just two different people. No big deal, it happens all of the time. At least, I thought it was no big deal.

At 8:30AM the next day, a Saturday, my phone rang. Now, I don't know about you, but I like to sleep in on Saturdays and Sundays and I don't know anybody who would call me that early, as even telemarketers have to wait until nine. Oh wait, I knew exactly who it would be, Tracy, so I didn't answer the phone.

"It's Tracy," went the venomous message on my machine. "It's obvious from the way you behaved last night that you have no interest at all in Marcia. Call me so we can talk about it. CLICK."

Yeah, I'm going to rush to return that phone call. It's bad enough that she made it clear that she was mad, but to wake me up to yell at me, that's just wrong. Hell, even my ex-wife didn't do that!

I did call Tracy that night and I asked what she meant by "my behavior" making it clear that I didn't like her. She said that I "hardly ever got into any deep conversations with her," which means I didn't like her. So while I'm with a group of six and there are group conversations, I'm supposed to ignore everybody and just spend the night talking to Marcia? I thought it was a casual night where we just met, no pressure for anything to happen. HAH! I'm now in trouble because I didn't ignore everybody and spend the night staring googly-eyed at Marcia. I told Tracy that as soon as I said I was a Republican, it was clear that Marcia didn't want to talk to me and she rebuffed my attempts at private conversations. Of course, it then became my fault for injecting politics into the discussion, even though I didn't start the discussion. I just listened for another five minutes and then got off the phone. I didn't hear from Tracy and Paul for another six months.

See, for committing the horrible crime of not immediately falling in love, I was a bad guy. Tracy felt that I was attacking her by not liking her selection for me. It's not that Marcia was a bad person; it's that she wasn't a good match for me, but women are unable to see that point when they're attempting a fix-up. It becomes all about them and their need to be successful, rather than our need to select someone appropriate for us. Of course, it's also always the guy's fault. Tracy hadn't blamed Marcia for things not going well. Oh no, it was my fault for not sweeping her off her feet.

The plain fact is that nobody knows what attracts people to one another. Think of all of the couples that you know. I will bet that for most of them, you have said at one time or another, "I wonder what she sees in him." People are attracted to one another and find romance for dozens of reasons, from looks to occupation to dancing ability. And despite what Hugh Hefner says, breast size is not in the top five of the traits that guys consider. That's why people have to understand that most fix-ups will not work. It's not a reflection on them, or their noble desire to help us find romance; it's just the way of romance.

Guideline #16

Instant Attraction Is a Fairy Tale

Or

Why is She Marrying Him?

I think we've all run into this person. She believes in "love at first sight" and other Disney propaganda. Never mind that mutual love and respect can only come after you spend time getting to know each other. These people want Prince Charming to come along and magically sweep them off their feet, just as he did in the movies. In the real world, however, the five-minute Prince Charming always ends up being Prince Shallow. Here are some actual ads from a dating service, completely unedited:

"One look and you'll just know. It's so true isn't it?" (34 and never married)

"I'm a true believer in 'the spark.' I can tell within 5 minutes if I click with someone and that's all I look for. I'm very picky, but only because I don't like to waste anyone's time or my own. If I don't think there is chemistry from the start, I don't proceed." (38 and never married)

"I'm not sure what I'm looking for, to be honest. I know that as soon as I meet him, we'll know we were meant for each other." (43 and never married)

The woman who takes the instant attraction route is dooming herself to failure. Often, attraction leads us to precisely the type of person we should avoid. As with the Jerk Magnet, the "spark seeker" is continually selecting only one type of man, and then complaining that all men are the same. Attraction is great and can lead to a lot of great, but meaningless, sex. Love, which is the basis of every solid relationship, is different from attraction. Love is based on deeper qualities than a person's eye color, shoulder width, and initial pick-up line.

Instead of picking out a guy, think about picking out a house. You look at ten or fifteen houses and then one instantly grabs your eye. A five-minute walk-though shows off a nice interior, but doesn't let you check out the basement. Do you immediately buy the house? Of course you don't. You check out the neighborhood, the price, the schools, and the utility bills. Then, you have a home inspection because you don't know what might be hiding behind those freshly painted walls. It might grab your thoughts instantly, but the taxes might be high, the well water might be drying up, or there could be mold in the basement. You're about to make a major investment; of course you're going to check it out thoroughly. You don't want to waste your time or money and get stuck with a lemon. Yet when picking a potential mate some people are willing to base everything on that first five minutes and details be damned.

These women will waste thousands of emotional dollars on dates because they are unwilling to be thorough, to look behind the initial impression when selecting potential partners. In fact, that initial impression becomes your guide for happiness. No spark, no follow-through. No chance to learn more about someone and no chance to learn more about yourself.

I'm not just speaking about appearance either, because I know that personality has a big influence on women's initial attraction (men are another story). What grabs your attention is not always what holds your attention. And just because it grabs your attention doesn't mean it's worthwhile. It's an axiom that you follow in every other area of life; why not follow it here too?

Let's apply the "instant spark" theory to buying clothes. When you're walking through Macys and you see an outfit that you love, do you immediately buy it? Nope. You look at the size, examine it for defects, and then will most likely try it on. Just because it looks good on the rack doesn't mean it will look good on you, so you've got to check to make sure that it doesn't make your thighs seem fat. You know that just because you're initially attracted to an outfit, it's not necessarily something you want in your wardrobe. Why wouldn't the same be true for a relationship, which is a much more important item in your life?

Spending your dating career looking for "the spark" leads to two things. First, it ensures that you meet the same type of person every time, whether you're aware of it or not. The same person, incidentally, that you've proven won't be right for you because you're still single. If instant attraction led to successful relationships, you would be in one. Here's a quote that appeared later in the profile of one of our daters quoted above:

"I tried using this service about a year ago but never met anyone that I was attracted to. I want to meet some new people and seem to be in a rut with the same network of friends."

She openly admits that she's in a rut with meeting the same people, but doesn't see that it's because she is severely limiting herself. She never bothered to follow through with anyone on the service because she's looking for the magical "instant attraction." That's the real problem with looking for a spark; it's not based on anything real. Attraction is fun, but not right. For example, think about these three things:

A hot fudge sundae with extra whipped cream.

Skydiving

Chevy Chase movies

They're all attractive at some point, but they're also not that good for you on a regular basis, even though it seems like they would be. No matter how hard we want it to be true, you just can't live on a steady diet of sundaes or Chevy Chase movies. It's the same with picking a romantic partner – we're usually attracted to the person who is not right or good for us. Attraction does not usually lead to affection and affection is what keeps a relationship going. Yet we continually refuse to change our dating patterns and so we continually pick the same person who is unable to give us what we really need to make a relationship last.

We all have friends who are really obvious about it. The woman who is always engaged but never marries or the guy who always has a date but never has a serious relationship.

This is one of those rare cases when both men and women will make the same mistake. I know you've heard it hundreds of times – "I really like her, but I'm not attracted to her, you know." For guys, it usually means the woman is overweight. For women, it usually means the guy is nerdy or unavailable.

Let's take a little deeper look at attraction. Think about the last two people who you *wanted* to date. Not necessarily dated, but wanted to date. In fact, it's probably better if you pick two people that you wanted to date but they didn't want to date you. Now write down the top five things that you can remember about that person. I'll use it for a girl I wanted a second date with and her deepest desire was to never see me again.

The first five things I remember about Amy:

1. Very pretty.

2. A sexy body.

3. A sense of humor.

4. Very pretty.

5. A sexy body.

An interesting list, but how many of those traits can be counted on in a relationship? The sense of humor is a help, but that's the only one. The others are nice to have, but not a guarantee of a long-term relationship. As Rodney Dangerfield said, "marry a good cook because the sex will wear off but you'll always be hungry."

Now, you obviously have to have some attraction. There's got to be a little spark. But that spark does not have to, and should not be, that instant heat that you remember from when you first saw David Cassidy or Farrah Fawcett.

There's a wonderful episode of *The Odd Couple* that addresses this very issue. Oscar's ex-wife Blanche is planning to remarry, but Felix protests the marriage because Blanche isn't "really in love." Felix defines love as being "that shortness of breath when the other person comes into the room," and adds more items that describe instant attraction. Oscar responds by saying, "that's love when you're 14 years old." Felix retorts, "then I am forever 14." Isn't that how we all feel at times? Yes, but as Oscar correctly realizes, there is so much more to love than that and there are so many different ways to express love that relying on the "instant spark" approach is incredibly damaging.

The plain fact is that this instant spark rarely exists and when you do find it, it's always in the beginning of relationships that don't last. That spark is an instinctual response based on physical and psychological characteristics that we don't understand or recognize. It's not what you base a relationship upon and the lack of it doesn't mean that a relationship is doomed.

I have had a lot of women argue this point with me and the ironic thing is that all of them are single. Women love the concept of that "instant spark." Let me explain how "instant spark" works for a guy and not a woman. The instant spark for a guy is 99% based on sex appeal and so when a woman responds to us because of that instant spark, our goal is to get her in bed. When we do, we then start thinking about the other stuff, like a relationship. Many times we will go through the motions of a relationship in order just to get sex. When that need is satisfied with this woman, we end the relationship. Usually before that happens, the woman realizes that we're only in it for sex and she ends the relationship, deeply hurt. Fortunately, men start to grow out of their side of it in their thirties, as we realize that it takes more then sex to make us happy. Many women, however, continue to search for that spark because to a woman, the spark is not entirely about sex. It's still not about what you need, however.

Guideline #17

Men Need Clear, Specific Directions (and I Don't Mean While Driving)

Or

Just Tell Me What You Want!

"I've told him a thousand times, but he never changes." How many times have you said that about a guy? That's because men and women communicate in fundamentally different ways. Men communicate in a linear and visual manner. Only God knows how women communicate.

If you want to see how men communicate, watch how we interact with each other. Our communications are short, blunt, and usually to the point. It might be a stupid point, but we usually get there right away. Look at a common guy's cheer in baseball, "Yankees suck." Short, to the point, and it encompasses everything that we believe. There's no need to give examples, to discuss what others think, or even to search deep within ourselves for the origin of that thought. The fact that the Yankees suck is something we know with every fiber of our being.

When we address each other, it's not with meaningless endearments, it's with pithy nicknames like "Stinky," "Retard," and "Dumbass." When a guy is mad at another guy, he makes sure to let the other guy know quickly and easily. When somebody calls you a dumbass, you know he thinks you've done something stupid. There is no innuendo involved in arguments among men. That's why we will sometimes end up using our fists - we're a little too clear about how we feel about each other.

Women are the exact opposite in their communication and anger. They will use misdirection and guile as they deliberately try and confuse you. Two women can be mad at each other for years and never exchange a cross word. They will "know" that the other is mad at them and continue on that path. All of their sniping will be done to others.

Look at how most arguments start between men and women. After the woman spends a few days acting cold, the man will ask if there's something wrong. We then get the basic response, "you know why I'm mad." That leaves us only two options and neither is pretty. We can pretend we know and try and bluff our way through it or we can openly admit we don't know what we've done wrong and then take double abuse for "being so blind as to not know when you've done something wrong."

See, we're like a dog. You've got to catch us in the act and rub our noses in it; otherwise, we just proceed on through life as if everything's fine. If you see a dog take a crap on the rug, you let him know right away it's bad. When a boyfriend does something wrong, women add it to a mental ledger that eventually spills out like Vesuvius.

Women will constantly make fun of men for memorizing thousands of sports statistics, movie lines, and strip bar locations as filling our minds with useless information. They will then taunt men, asking, "why do you fill your head with all of that stupid crap?" Women can't fill their minds with sports trivia because their minds are filled with thoughts of relationships. If we look at brains like a collection of file boxes, men's file boxes are filled with movies and sports teams. Women's file boxes are filled with relationship details. If we're at a baseball game discussing light-hitting shortstops, our brain pulls out the Mark Belanger file. A woman will go to her relationship file box and pull out the file of the baseball game when you had too many beers and belched in her face. A guy will say, "remember the year Mark Belanger hit .287?" but you'll never hear a guy ask, "remember what you said to me last August?" Women will say that at least once a year. In fact, every guy reading this book has forgotten everything I've said and is trying to figure out if Mark Belanger really did hit .287 (yes, in 1969).

If you really want to get along with a man, tell him right away when he makes a mistake or does something you don't like. That's how we learn what you like. Please, please, don't use that tired old line, "anyone would know how to act in that situation," because we obviously don't or we would have acted that way. Why in the world would you want to hide how you feel? Tell us, we'll all be better off.

We need to know exactly everything you want and how you want it. If you want flowers for your anniversary, then tell us you want flowers. Don't say "anything will be fine" and then pout because you didn't get flowers. Let us know and we'll do what you want. Why wouldn't you want to do that?

Let me give you two quick examples. Monday morning you try a new route to work and traffic is horrible and it takes you twenty minutes longer to get to work. The same thing happens Tuesday and Wednesday mornings. What route do you take to work on Thursday? The old one, of course.

Example two. You've been with a guy for three years and Christmas time is quickly approaching. The first year you were dating he got you a crystal cat for Christmas. Granted, you like cats, but it wasn't anything you really wanted. The second year was a little better in that he got you a pretty necklace and matching earrings, but it wasn't the leather jacket that you really wanted and still want this year. What will you do when he asks you what you want for Christmas this year? Will you say something like "surprise me," or "anything is fine?" Will you tell him the exact coat you want? I bet you don't and I know you'll be disappointed, again.

What's the difference between the two examples? In both of them, the same action produces the same result. Yet in the first example you will change your behavior to achieve the desired result. It's what everybody does. Why in a relationship would you expect the result to change when your behavior does not change? Why are you surprised when the result doesn't change? And why is it our fault for not changing when you don't change either? If you want something specific from a guy, tell us specifically what you want.

This also applies to sex. If you like to have the back of your neck kissed, tell us. We'll do it. Heck, we'll do anything you want. We're so happy to be having sex that we will try to please you.

Granted, there are guys who are not interested in pleasing the woman at all. But then, why would you stay with a guy like that?

I've had several women say to me (none of them whom I had sex with, by the way) that men don't "know their way around the clitoris." Of course we don't, we don't have one and we haven't had the chance to see as many as we'd like to see. I asked these women if they ever told the guys what they wanted and they all said no. Some of them even faked orgasms so as not to let the guy know that he wasn't doing it right. How in the world can any guy improve if you don't tell us what we're doing wrong, and even worse, reward us for doing the wrong thing? Tell us what you want us to do with your clitoris, believe me, we absolutely want you to enjoy sex and have orgasms. Not because we care about your feelings, but because we know that if you enjoy sex, you'll want to have more of it and that's what we really like!

Please, please don't use the line, "it's not the same if I have to ask for it" because that's you putting a false expectation on other people. If you like occasional gifts, then let us know something you'd like. Let us know when you'd like it. Our not remembering doesn't mean that we don't love you.

Not only that, but women will not verbalize their needs and then get mad at the man for not satisfying their needs. "He knew by my expressions that I didn't like it," assumes that we know every nuance of your expressions. We don't read books, how in the world do you expect us to read your face? Tell us so that we can fix it, don't remain quiet or obfuscate your answer in order to test us.

That's where it gets really tricky, when you use our inaction to define our love, or lack thereof. You'll create an imaginary test for us, "if he remembers the anniversary of our first date, then I'll know he cares," or some other nonsense like that. If we don't know it's a test, we can't pass. At some point every guy will fail that test because we don't know the rules. In fact, if you find yourself giving tests like this, you need to re-examine the relationship and your need to sabotage it.

If communication is the key to a relationship, and we all believe it is, then that communication must be open and direct. That's what men understand and what we need. The greatest way of making sure your needs are met is to tell us exactly what they are and exactly how we can satisfy them.

Guideline #18

Settling is Good

Or

Things Change, Deal With It

I know it seems like a lot, but I'm not settling for anything less. – Match.com quote

I want it all. – Julia Roberts in *Pretty Woman*

People tell me I have high standards but I'm not going to lower them now so if you don't meet all of the above, don't bother writing. – Match.com quote

I'm still waiting for my knight in shining armor. – Yahoo Personals quote

Missed it by that much! – Maxwell Smart

By thirty, the traditional male career dreams of athletics

and success have either come true or not come true enough to force us to reevaluate and adjust. When women haven't reached their personal dreams by thirty as they relate to relationships, they often refuse to admit that their dreams are unrealistic. There just aren't a ton of guys who are:

- Athletic yet don't like to watch sports

- Confident, yet not arrogant

- Good looking

- Charming

- Have successful careers yet leave work at 5pm every day

The hope of meeting this ideal mate is still there and rather than re-evaluate, as most men do, these unrealistic standards become hardened in women's souls. In their minds, it's not a problem with the standards, but a problem of "not having met the right guy yet." It's everybody's fault but hers. The impossible list of traits that they have been accumulating since viewing Sleeping Beauty are still valid in their minds and to accept any less than that ideal would be "settling." The focus switches from whether or not their dreams are realistic to the fact that most men do not meet their dreams. It becomes a failure of the men she's dating. It's their fault for not meeting her often impossible ideal and so she builds up anger towards men for failing her.

While many of you may try to dismiss this by saying it's just a few women or by saying that your ideal man is realistic, this concept of mine was confirmed by a recent article in *Psychology Today*. It discussed depression in many of today's women. One of the conclusions was that women, especially those in their thirties and beyond, have extremely long and complicated traits that they expect their potential partners to possess. The article went on to discuss how these expectations are so high that they are usually unmet, leaving women bitter, angry, and depressed. It's enough of a trend that Psychology Today was preparing mental health professionals to deal with it on a regular basis. That anger and bitterness among women is not new information to most of us single men who are active daters, as we hear angry women all the time. A lot of that talk is about how they're "not settling for less than I deserve."

You'll even hear women discuss this all of the time amongst themselves and all over the media. It's a point of pride among some women, "I'm not settling!" The gist of the argument is that as a worthwhile person she deserves to have everything that she wants in a man. To accept anything even slightly different or "less than perfect" in her eyes is to demean herself and her worth. It's as if she is saying, "I am wonderful and I am strong and so I must have all my needs fulfilled." The first part of that statement is great, women should be strong and proud and happy with themselves. It's the second part of that statement that is completely and utterly ridiculous.

No one in the world, not even Bill Gates, gets everything he wants. They especially don't get everything that they believe they deserve. The plain truth is that we, as human beings, are forced to "settle" in every aspect of our life every day. There is nothing wrong with the concept. It's called compromise and it is how the world works. Nobody gets everything they want in anything. Why do women somehow think that they should not only get everything they fantasize about in a man, but that they somehow **deserve** it?

I have always dreamed of living in a house near a woods and stream. It's something I've fantasized about since I was a kid. The thought of being able to relax and take a walk out the back door and listen to a stream gurgle is something that makes me smile. It's what I've always wanted in a house. However, when I went to buy my first house I couldn't afford the house by the stream. So I bought a great townhouse and loved living in it. I could have stayed there for the rest of my life, but after 17 years I had an improved financial picture and I decided to move. Yep, I looked at a house or two that was next to a stream. They weren't as nice as some of the other houses I saw and as I thought about what was important to me, a stream just wasn't as vital to my happiness as how the other houses made me feel. So I ended up buying a wonderful house that had a beautiful yard that backed onto a small forest, but there's no stream. I love my new house and I couldn't be happier. I don't even think about the stream that I wanted for a long time because it's not as important as finding something that made me happy. It didn't meet my dreams, but it met my needs and wants and desires. This house warms my soul when I think of it, stream or no stream. The stream, like six-pack abs, wasn't something really important. I settled for less than my dream house, but I couldn't be happier with my decision.

Let's go even smaller. I'd love to eat my lunch out every day and have a nice dessert with that lunch. A nice cold cut sub, some fries, and chocolate cake would be perfect. I'd love to have a similar lunch every day and I can afford it financially. I'd also end up being 800 pounds and they'd have to bury me in a piano case. I compromise and have that lunch once a week. It may be my dream to have it every day, but that's **not realistic or healthy**, so I compromise.

Look at every aspect of your life – clothes, furniture, car – are they everything that you have dreamed of and deserve? Of course not! I'd love to wear nice Ralph Lauren shirts, have lush carpeting and drive a Jaguar. Is any of that going to happen? Maybe the carpeting will happen at some point. That does not mean that I have a bad life or I'm a bad person or somehow have done something to injure myself. The sign of an intelligent, well-adjusted person is the ability to adapt to circumstances. You don't wear a bathing suit to the opera and you don't buy a house you can't afford. That doesn't make you less of a person or doom you to an unfulfilled life. It actually allows you to live.

The myth of settling is of course promoted by the media, especially Hollywood and Cosmopolitan. They're busy telling everybody that you can have it all and it's not even that hard to get it.

Let's look at one of my favorite examples again, the movie *Pretty Woman*. Do you remember the scene at the end when Roberts and Gere break up? Women get deeply affected by this scene. Gere offers to set her up in an apartment or make some other arrangement so that they can still be together and Roberts turns him down because it's not enough for her. She wants it all and he smiles knowingly and leaves because he's really not able to give her everything she wants.

I know it's a movie, but let's recap her decision. She rejects life as a billionaire's girlfriend, with the possibility of advancement to wife, to return to the life of a whore. After ten days, she demands marriage from a guy who has spent an entire lifetime avoiding commitment and that's a rational and logical choice for her? She'll return to degrading herself and selling loveless sex to pathetic men rather then continue to date and romance a man with whom she finds a connection. The crazy thing is that women applaud her choice. They nod in agreement when she implies that she needs marriage immediately. She needs it all and she needs it **now**.

I realize that this conflict is necessary to create the dramatic ending of the movie and I do enjoy the movie. Garry Marshall did a great job with it and he should be proud of it. The problem is that women are relating to the exact wrong message in the movie.

Forget about the myth that a whore is as clean and pretty as Julia Roberts. The women that see this movie all believe that she did the right thing in "not settling." Women actually believe that her "no settling" stance led to Gere arriving with opera music playing, waving roses. After all, if she hadn't "held out" for it all, she wouldn't have gotten it. What she wanted was an **unrealistic fairy tale**, a Hollywood ending, not real life. Since this was a Hollywood movie, she got it. In the original script, Gere didn't come back and when Roberts got back to her apartment, her roommate had OD'd from the drugs she bought with the money she had been given by Roberts. That's real life. Women still treat that Hollywood ending as something that is not just possible, but probable. They're looking for that fairy tale to envelop them and wash away reality.

Now I can hear all of you women objecting right now. "You're telling me to put up with anything just so I'm not alone" and other comments not quite as nice as that. That is not what I'm saying at all. What I'm saying is that dreams do not always translate into reality and it's not reality's fault. It's not my fault either. It's not the fault of the guy you're on a date with either. He is who he is and it's wrong to be angry or disappointed with him because he's not who you wish he would be. Rigid adherence to unrealistic and unreasonable standards can produce nothing but bitterness.

Think about your standards right now. Are they realistic? Can they possibly apply to more than two people in the entire country? If those same standards were applied to you, would you meet them? Are you eliminating decent people because they don't meet every single characteristic on your list? Are his physical characteristics more important than his emotional ones? Do you meet the same standard for physical characteristics that you insist upon?

I'm reminded of a story from television (of course) that fits this situation. When Selma and Sideshow Bob are about to marry on *The Simpsons*, Selma becomes upset and wants to break off the engagement when she finds out Bob doesn't like *MacGyver*. He didn't like something that was important to her and so that was it as far as she was concerned. Homer saves the impending marriage by telling Bob to go to the bar when she watches MacGyver. Or, as my brother says, "two TVs can save a marriage." Your intended does not have to love everything you do in order for him to be a great match. Nor do you have to love everything about him.

It's called compromise. Yeah, it'd be great if your boyfriend loved to go to craft shows and antique fairs, but if he doesn't, don't disqualify him. The same goes for appearances. Women are appalled and disgusted when they hear men talk about how they love women with big breasts. If a man only dates women with big breasts, he's a fool and would be told he's a fool by his friends. If a woman requires a certain height or six-pack abs in a date, she's just as big a fool, but her girlfriends will agree with her and tell her not to settle. She doesn't want to "settle" for a guy who's not her physical ideal, so why should she bother getting to know him?

Talk to your married friends and see if their first date matched their initial "dream date." Chances are their initial impression was not that of perfection. A lot of them even met them as friends first. Their spouses have flaws and they accept them and work around them because they have flaws too. We all do. Accepting others' flaws is part of being human and to expect people to be flawless and everything to go flawless is unrealistic and is damaging to your soul.

As we age, we also tend to be less accepting of flaws and differences. When you're 22, you accept that your date loves to watch football, assuming he'll grow out of it. When he doesn't, you've had a few years to get used to it and it rarely bothers you. If you were to start dating the exact same guy at 35, you'd have to accept that he's going to watch football and you find that very difficult. You fight it and him because it doesn't match what you want, when it's most likely something that you can accept and work around IF you are willing to put forth some effort.

Think about what you really want in a mate. Not the superficial things that you probably think about, but what you really need to make you happy. Does their occupation, ability to dance, or amount of body fat really have anything to do with what makes a satisfying relationship? You want somebody that makes you happy and treats you with respect and love. Everything else can be worked out.

Guideline #19

Children are the Ultimate Deal-Breaker

Or

I Hate the Thought of the Pitter-Patter of Little Feet

At our age, the major stumbling block in most relationships is children. Either you want them or you don't, and if you want them, you generally have them. If you're over 35 and indifferent about children, that means that you've also made a decision, though you might not admit it. These "children camps" collide all of the time and that leads to chaos as we try to adapt our views to fit the person whom we like.

Let's start with the obvious first: people who have children. They live in a different world from people who don't have children, though they don't realize it. I went to a party at my brother's house a year or so ago and I was the only person there who didn't have children. What were the conversation topics? You guessed it – sports leagues, school strategies, day care, and

playtimes. There were five different groups having conversations

and every single one of their conversations concerned parenting.

All of the subjects are things that a single person can't relate to in

the slightest. So what happens? Childless people stop hanging

around parents and vice versa, so the problem gets worse, not

better. The parents are clueless that they're cutting us out of their

conversations, but every childless person hears the same two things

all the time from parental units – "If you had kids, you'd

understand," and "you have to have kids, they're wonderful."

See, parents just can't understand why everyone else

doesn't want what they want. It colors their judgment in every

situation because they can't comprehend why you don't want to

talk about children. It starts with the old "you have to come see the

baby" and never stops. Even people who like kids tend to avoid

these situations because there's nothing in them to which we can

relate.

I have a married friend and he and his wife choose not to have children, which is a perfectly fine choice. I have been present on numerous occasions when he and/or his wife have been lectured, berated, and openly pitied by parents for their decision to remain childless, even when it's something that they both want. Every one of those conversations ends with, "you just can't imagine how wonderful kids are," as if having kids is a miraculous cure-all. The plain truth is that people who don't want kids shouldn't have kids. In fact, many people who have kids shouldn't have kids. People that don't want kids do not make good parents, so let's applaud people that don't want children and live that choice.

Now, the above example is the extreme kind, people who have kids hanging out with people who don't want kids. It's a guaranteed failure. Ninety percent of the people involved in those situations realize it and so they only date like-minded people.

There are people who have kids who can successfully date people who want kids, but even that has its own obstacles. The most obvious one is the child or children who already exist. That child has an enormous say in the relationship and by his behavior can completely sabotage an otherwise fine relationship. It's a tough situation because a parent has to respect a child, but that child can dislike a potential partner just because they are a potential partner.

It can also go overboard. I once went on a date with a divorced mom of a seven-year-old boy. I got dumped because I hadn't seen "The Mummy." Really. It was a movie that the two of them watched all the time and since I didn't know it, she didn't think that I'd fit in with her family life. Was she right or wrong? I don't know, but right or wrong, it's an example of my saying that children are the ultimate deal-breaker.

Next up is a situation that is sad and frustrating, that of the woman who doesn't have children, yet wants them. There's nothing wrong with that, but when that urge gets so intense that it becomes your primary goal in life, it is wrong. It means you're picking a man so that you can have children, not because he's the right person for you or your future family.

I was in early contact with someone from eHarmony and here are a couple of things that she said. The one thing she was most passionate about was "the importance of family." The most important thing she was looking for in a mate was "Someone who can provide a caring, stable environment for a family." The dream she most wanted to come true was "to quit my job and become a stay at home mom." And finally, the first question she had for me was, "As we get older our time lines change. How long do you date someone before you consider marriage?" Wow, that's a woman with an agenda. The only good part about that would be you know she'd never insist on using a condom.

It's not necessarily a bad agenda unless the person decides that it's more important to find someone to have children with, then to find a life partner. Sounds like I'm splitting hairs, but if your ultimate goal in relationship hunting is to have children, then you're making a mistake. And yes, I realize that as a man, I don't know what it's like to have that incredible maternal urge. I don't know that, but I do know the result of relationships that are based primarily on having children immediately and it's not good.

With all of our political correctness and "understanding," we seem to have forgotten that children are supposed to be the result of a loving relationship, not a goal in and of itself. The relationship must be primary. Children are not something that you have for you; you have them for them and to spread the joy and love of a successful relationship, not the unfulfilled dreams of a lonely person. A child is a separate person with her own dreams, goals and lives, not an extension of your life or a person to live out the life that you didn't. A lot of men don't understand that either – they're the ones who insist on naming their child after themselves, the ultimate narcissism.

I can only imagine how hard it must be for women who find themselves in the Scratch and Dent Section, desperately seeking someone to have children with. That biological clock must be ticking loudly and it must be frustrating to watch others achieve the families that you've always desired for yourself. However, by focusing on children (and mentioning them insistently in your initial conversations), you're severely damaging your chances to find the right person.

Tracy was a woman that contacted me through Match.com. She was 42, cute, and had an interesting profile. Her initial contact was brief, just saying that she was interested and that I should e-mail her if I was interested. I was, so I sent her an e-mail, asking her a couple of questions about things she had mentioned in her profile (job, movies, etc.). Her response, "Do you really want to waste time discussing this via e-mail? Call me if you have the strength to move quickly on a great thing." Imagine that, not being willing to spend time getting to know each other via e-mail when you've joined **an internet dating service**!

I reviewed her profile again and immediately found the problem. She was 42, put that having children was "a must," and she was "unwilling to adopt." Hmmmm, think she was in a hurry to have children? Imagine putting that kind of pressure on yourself. Imagine putting that pressure on someone in your very first e-mail to them. Her anger and frustration at being 42 and childless were painfully obvious in her accusation directed towards me about whether or not I had strength. It's not weakness that causes a person to not move forward, but she had already determined that it was my failure and issue if I didn't want to immediately call her. Her idea of a relationship was based solely on her desire for children quickly and it had warped into the fault of all single men. Yeah, that's somebody I'm going to move forward with.

In a way, I felt sorry for Tracy, as everything about her cried out, "I want children and I'm getting too old to have them." It must be an incredibly difficult situation for women, wanting exactly what you can't have, especially when society is also putting pressure on you to do what you'd love to do. However, you can not let that pressure force you into making a relationship choice. If there's one thing that should not be rushed, it's parenting.

Relationships have a natural ebb and flow and they do take time. Attempting to speed things up, not because of your attraction to the person, but because of a desire to have children, is a colossal mistake.

Guideline #20

There Are Some Guys Who Must Be Avoided

Or

Stay the Heck Away!

I've done a lot of bashing on women in this book, so it's time to talk trash about guys. The plain truth is that there are a lot of guys out there who should not be dated because of their flaws. I guess they can be dated by someone who is also flawed, and they usually are, but a lot of times women have trouble seeing these men for what they truly are – undateable idiots. The bits of their personality that they show are often closely intertwined with characteristics that appeal to women, so they will be initially appealing. If you can learn to spot these guys at the start, you can avoid yourself a lot of heartache. That is, if you're looking for a real, fulfilling relationship. If all you want is a brief, unfulfilling relationship, then ignore my advice and date them. In fact, you probably already do that.

Mr. Competitive

To this guy, everything is a competition that must be played all out. An office softball game, tossing a Frisbee at the beach, or the seventh game of the World Series are all the same to this guy – to be played at maximum speed and with maximum destructive force. He's the guy who dives into a small boy's sandcastle at the beach because he's got to make "the catch" while playing Frisbee with his nephew. The kind of guy who knocks down the elderly second baseman to break up a double play during a casual game of softball. Moderation isn't in this guy's vocabulary, if he plays, he plays to win at all costs. When someone complains about his arrogant style of play, he'll usually toss out Leo Doroucher's quote, "nice guys finish last." He loves to mock the people that he competes against and the concept of winning gracefully is lost on him.

Initially this guy can be very attractive to women. That super-competitive edge can lead to success in business and sports, both of which women find appealing. Plus, that competitive arrogance also draws women, as he is very forward in dealing with them. There's still an element in woman's DNA that attracts them to the male who wins at competition and these guys know it and exploit it. His indifference and then pursuit can greatly intrigue and captivate a woman at first.

However, this guy needs to be avoided at all costs because that super-competitiveness cannot be turned on and off. The same arrogant way in which he treats his co-workers and co-competitors is the same way in which he will treat you and your family. Mr. Competitive is so competitive because underneath all of that arrogance is a frightened little boy who must win to gain approval. That frightened boy can only feel good when he's triumphing over someone else. Compromise or losing means weakness and that can't be shown. A man who can't allow himself to be weak also is unable to participate in an equal, shared relationship.

It's easy to spot Mr. Competitive, he's the guy who:

- Wears spikes during the office softball game.

- Plays in at least three different leagues of the same sport at the same time.

- Spends more than fifty dollars for a baseball bat.

- Always manages to accidentally tackle somebody during a touch football game.

- Challenges people to race or arm wrestle.

- Taunts people.

- Drives a red Camaro.

- Still wears his high school sports jacket.

- Owns multiple jerseys of his favorite sports team.

The Jerk

Now I've discussed the jerk in detail in several other chapters, so I'll be brief here. Jerks are to be avoided at all costs. It's easy to tell a jerk, just look at how he treats other people. Not you. Not people that he needs to get something from. How does he treat people who are powerless to take action against him? If the answer is badly, he's a jerk, plain and simple, and needs to be avoided at all costs.

The Obsessive Sports Fan

Actually, obsessiveness is to be avoided in all things, but for some reason, obsessiveness tends to be accepted in sports fans. The fact is that anyone who spends all of their time following a sports team is someone that will eventually start ignoring you. It's okay to be a big sports fan, but watch out for the following:

- His car radio is always set to an AM sports talk station and at least one of the talk show hosts calls him a regular.
- He wears authentic player jerseys to places other than games.
- He writes long and angry comments on local sports blogs.
- He doesn't play any of the sports he follows.
- Personal grooming is way down on his list of priorities.
- During games, he screams at players, even though he's in the upper deck.
- He still hates Bill Buckner (New England sports fans only)

One thing to note about the obsessive sports fan is that he usually became an obsessive sports fan because he couldn't get laid. That energy got transferred to sports and now he's just angry and bitter about his team. However, losing all of that

anger and bitterness is incredibly difficult and they should be
avoided.

The Slickee Boy

The Slickee Boy is oftentimes considered the ideal mate.
Well-dressed, immaculate manners, perfect grooming, and being
outgoing make this guy seem like a dream date. In fact, he would
be a dream date if what you were seeing were not an elaborately
crafted illusion. The Slickee Boy doesn't behave and appear the
way he wants, he has crafted the person he needs to be to get what
he wants.

In the past few years, the media has latched onto this
personality type, calling them Metrosexuals. What a horrible name,
because it doesn't imply that there's something wrong with their
behavior. Their incredible narcissism needs to be implicit in their
name, hence Slickee Boy. Remember, I'm not saying that there's
something wrong with being stylish. However, when the style

becomes the main point or the central focus, you move from the area of great guy to Slickee Boy.

A Slickee Boy always wears classic clothes from top-of-the-line stores. No Marshall's for a Slickee Boy, his ties are Brooks Brothers and his socks are from Barney's. He moves seamlessly in the corporate world, always wearing the appropriate uniform. When he's off work, the Slickee Boy likes to wear his sweater tied around the neck of his Ralph Lauren Polo Shirt. He's a step up from a car salesman, but you can't trust anything either of them has to say.

Confidence? The Slickee Boy has plenty of it. When he's unwinding with his officemates during Happy Hour, the Slickee Boy will be sure to have a funny story to tell, entertaining everybody. That story, however, will always rely on someone else being the sap. That's the true way to tell a Slickee Boy, he's unable to laugh at himself. Since everything about him is a charade, with no substance or foundation, laughing at himself means the charade isn't working and that can't be admitted.

It's why you always see the Slickee Boy with dates and girlfriends, but very few of them ever advance to marriage. With the real person hidden by the Slickee Construct, there's nothing for him to share with his partner and he's unable to be emotionally intimate because he has no idea of his true emotions. Oh, the Slickee boy will eventually marry, when it becomes important to maintain the image. He'll find a pretty woman of appropriate social standing and they'll have a lovely wedding with a honeymoon at Sandals. By fifty, he'll be near the top of the corporate ladder and his wife will be a closet alcoholic.

The signs of a Slickee Boy:

- He drives the same car as his boss.

- He keeps up with his college fraternity.

- He loves to sail and has Lands End sailing clothes, rather than cut-offs and a beat up pair of tennis shoes.

- When he wears shorts, they have perfect creases.

- Favorite sport – golf.

- His part is always straight and his hair never gets out of place.

- His favorite sports teams are the Washington Redskins and Chicago Bulls.

- He spends more on grooming products than you do.

- He owns a comb and brush set.

- He works in sales.

The Super-nerd

First, it's important to distinguish between a super-nerd and an ordinary nerd because there's nothing wrong with dating an ordinary nerd. An ordinary nerd likes science fiction and is not good at sports. A super-nerd has memorized the dialogue from every episode of Star Trek (original and Next Generation) and can't even catch a Frisbee. A nerd is anxiously looking to make new friends and when he socializes will be able to carry on a relatively normal conversation. A super-nerd gets consistently tongue-tied and most of his relationships are one-sided affairs with models and porn stars. He's the guy who sends birthday cards to Jenna Jameson.

We've all known the super-nerd, in that they're completely socially inadequate and awkward. They've never learned to dress or groom themselves and they are generally unable to speak under pressure. The super-nerd is usually found alone or with an entire group of super-nerds, as nobody but other super-nerds will hang out with them. The reason for that is simple; they have no idea of how to handle social intercourse. Or any other kind of intercourse, but that's a different story.

Some super-nerd signs:

- He owns a ton of celebrity porn.
- He is very uncoordinated.

- He doesn't have any favorite sports teams because he doesn't like any sports.

- He buys Anime DVDs from Japan.

- He has set up multiple identities on websites so that he can argue with people anonymously.

- He watches a lot of E! and Court TV

- He's a multiple-day Jeopardy champion

- He has a ton of brilliant ideas but none of them have ever made it past the planning stage

- You won't want to talk to him.

Again, it's important to remember that it's a matter of degree, as a nerd isn't a bad candidate for a relationship, but a super-nerd is not. As a matter of fact, it's nerds who rule the world. Nerds control computers, banks, the media, and a ton of other industries. One characteristic of a nerd is that he's smart and he's able to successfully turn his brain to the real world, which a super-nerd is completely unable to do.

A nerd is actually an excellent candidate to date. Nerds are smart, he knows how to treat people because he knows what it's like to be treated badly, and he will usually have money. In fact, nerds will treat women like queens because they generally go without dates, so whenever they get a date they spend a lot of time making sure they do the right thing. Why do you think Ric Ocasek's marriage to Pavlina Porizkova has lasted longer than most celebrity marriages? She realized the value of dating a nerd. The nerd's desire to do the right thing also ensures that they'll do a lot of things that you ask them to do, which again makes them exactly the kind of guy women won't date, because they don't like guys who do what they ask them to do. Give it a try though, dating a nerd can be quite rewarding.

A Few More Words About Online Dating

Or

What Were You Thinking When You Posted That?

There are a ton of online dating services and I've briefly mentioned the two biggies, eHarmony and Match.com, elsewhere in the book so I don't want to get into specifics about how to succeed on either service. Both sites do feature auxiliary businesses that will "improve" your profile and make you a more popular date but you have to pay extra for that. I won't even mention the irony of eHarmony, which claims to match you up perfectly with people and also claims that if you pay more them to write your profile that you'll be more successful. Doesn't the one refute the other? Anyway, there's no need to pay a complete stranger to rewrite your profile. As a complete stranger I will give you some basic tips that will make you more appealing.

For god's sake have someone take a couple of photos of you! I'm constantly stunned at the number of people on both sites who use as their primary photo a picture that they took of themselves by holding the camera away from their body and pointed at their face. Quite a few people even have self-shot photos as their only photos. There is no way that this can be a flattering portrait of you. Not only are you physically at an odd angle but there's always some bland or boring background behind you and you end up making celebrity mug shots more appealing than your photo. When you have mostly or solely self-shot photos it also sends the message out that you don't have any friends. It's saying that you don't have anyone that you trust to take a photo of you and that you haven't been anywhere fun where others have taken photos of you. It also gives out a subtle message of anger because almost universally the person in a self-shot photo is not smiling. So ask a friend to take a picture of you and, for God's sake, if you're going to have them take multiple photos, don't have them all in the same room with you wearing the same outfit. I have seen numerous profiles of women where the only photos are five shots of them taken two seconds apart. You don't have to go on a glamour shoot but at least switch rooms and backgrounds. Have a friend take a couple of photos of you and then ask them which two are best and post them. Don't argue or complain, just post the ones that someone other than you has selected.

A few more photo tips and I'll start with one for the guys. Wear a shirt. I don't care if you're Hugh Jackman; wear a shirt in your main profile photo. You can mix in one or two bathing suit shots if you want but be clothed in your main photo. Just as importantly, don't pose in front of your car and please don't be decked out in apparel of your favorite sports team. For women the rules are slightly different; no photos with you on your horse or holding your cat, dog, or infant relative. We know you like cats and babies – you're a girl.

That's the main guideline – your primary photo should be mainly of you. It should also be in focus, recent, mostly a close-up, and feature nothing odd or unusual. Don't have it a picture shot from fifty feet away where all we can see is a faint blur. Nobody

wants to see you parachuting, scuba diving, jumping, driving, or

bungee jumping. I know. You want to show everybody that you're

not some stick-in-the-mud and that you're fun so you're going to

show them right at the start that you're an active, fun person.

That's great if we're picking out players for a sports team but no

one really cares about that when selecting a date. It also shouldn't

be you in a group or a picture that is obviously from an event

where someone is touching you and they're cropped out of the

picture but their arm around your waist is still there. Use those

pictures as secondary pictures if you must but try to keep the

majority of the pictures of just you. I also strongly advise women

not to post photos of them with other women around them. I

guarantee you that every guy who looks at a picture of three girls is

looking at all three of them, not just you, and he'll find a reason

why at least one of the other girls is more attractive.

    When writing your profile you should never mention how

you're reluctant to try online dating. I would say that at least half of the profiles I've read over the years open with something like, "I never thought I'd be trying online dating but Julie finally talked me into it." What you're really saying is, "I never thought I'd be as pathetic as you but I finally realized that I am alone and desperate." It's an online world and we don't need to waste time on your telling us how you didn't want to do this. Nobody does, so just man up and get on with it.

Stop trying to impress everybody with your wide range of activities and interests. According to most dating profiles nobody watches TV or eats at McDonalds. Think about all of the activities that you have listed and how often you have really done them. Is it a regular, monthly activity? If not, I would probably leave it out. I know that you're trying to toss out all your lures in the hopes that one item will attract somebody but instead it just becomes a buzz of busy-ness. Think of what you do in a typical month and put those activities in there. Don't try to put a glossy shine on it either – if you have skied once in the past ten years don't claim that you're an expert skier. Most of us enjoy a lot of things but we don't do most of them on a regular basis so stick to what you do regularly. It's also okay if you like to watch TV.

Try very hard to be yourself in your profile while also realizing that you are unique and you need to feature that. Try not to have a profile that sounds exactly like every other profile on your service. If you can, read some of the other profiles of people like you on the service. I would say that 80% of the profiles that I read online sound identical. Everybody is busy, happy, and loves to go out while also enjoying a quiet night watching a DVD. Every woman is capable of going from jeans to an evening gown and has read *Eat, Pray, Love* and *The Girl With the Dragon Tattoo*. Every guy likes to work out. List one activity or thing that makes you smile. For me, it's rummaging through used bookstores looking for something new or different or the fact that I make the best brownies in the world. I'm quite sure that you have something like that too so put it in there. Let us see the things that make you who you are, not the things that you think we want to read.

Keep all the anger out of your profile. We don't want to hear about your exes or how you're tired of "players" and "games." The part where you write about how you hate liars and want somebody you can trust – leave it out. You're telling everybody how you pick total idiots and have a seriously skewed radar. I can guarantee you that any woman who complains about players is a woman who picks guys based on instant attraction, not real qualities. It's the same with guys – don't complain about your clingy ex or how you're not looking for somebody. Everybody's on these dating services because they're looking for somebody. Even you.

Finding a Date That Satisfies Your Dream

Now I know what you're thinking – "Carl, if you know so much about relationships, why aren't you in one?" An excellent question. I wish I had an excellent answer, but the truth is that I find myself stuck in the same stupid patterns as those I point out. I am working on changing them, but, as you know, it is difficult.

The plain truth is, like most of us that are in our forties and single, I have several issues that I'm working on solving, but it's not as easy as I would like. I realize that recognizing patterns and then changing them is hard, but I am trying. My original plan was to have lots of sex to solve these issues, but that never really got off the ground, so to speak. So what did I do to try and break my patterns? The hardest thing of all, some therapy mixed in with self-reflection. I've also found that if you do honestly recognize your patterns, it does become easier to break them.

Several years ago I decided that the best way to try and break my patterns was to date every person who showed an interest in me. So I joined Match.com and went on dates with 22 different women in three months. Man was that a mistake! Actually, it wasn't, because it really helped me to see patterns in women and their needs and desires. It gave me a lot of material for this book, as I realized that almost every woman I've dated since my divorce has had an image of an ideal man in their head that they would compare with me. Men have a general idea of what they want, but it's nowhere near as specific as the image women carry. It's very hard to match up with this mythical image and so I decided to write this book to illustrate that no one is perfect and no one is a perfect date. . So how do you find that not-so-perfect-but-right-for-me date?

I've mentioned breaking patterns several times and it's easy for me to say that and very difficult for everyone, including me, to accomplish. Start by listing all the traits that you want in a partner. Search your soul to discover what would compliment it in a mate.

No wait, that's all bullcrap. The only way to break patterns is to open your mind a little bit. Relax those restrictions that you've put in place when assessing potential dates. Stop looking for Hugh Grant in *About a Boy* and start looking for a person who actually exists. If you're dating online, don't focus on the pictures and instead read the person's profile with a casual attitude. Don't search for specifics but try to find a feel for the real person. If that person sounds slightly attractive, take a look at his picture and if it's not horrible give him a try. You don't have to start dating him but open yourself to the possibility of dating him. Don't match them up against an imaginary checklist of traits and instead just see if they are a decent human being that might become a good friend. Allow them the chance to show you, and for you to show them, that a few flaws are okay because we all have them and we all live with them. Instead of going into dating by thinking of reasons to eliminate a person, try to find reasons to date him. It's always easy to find a reason to say no to somebody and you may be saying no to somebody who would be a good match for you.

The idea of a perfect mate is best left to the movies. A mate who can become your perfect match is possible in the real world if you drop your preconceived notions and concentrate on the core of a person. We all have flaws but that shouldn't stop us from getting out in the world and trying to find somebody that will be right for us. They may not match that dream date from our teenage years but they'll make a wonderful companion for all your years from here on.

It's my hope that now that you've read this book, your next dating experience might be a little different. Maybe you'll realize that just as it takes two to create a great date; it takes two to create a bad date. You can't change the way other people behave, but you can change the way you behave and the way you go about dating. Maybe it's time to try some new people and learn new ways of interacting. You might just find what you really want – that person who will love you and be wonderful to share the rest of your life with. Even if they don't own a house that's next to a stream or ski or have a perfect head of hair.

Actually, I wrote this for more than helping people find true love or improve their dating experiences. I really wrote it because I thought it would help me get laid.

Acknowledgements

This book never would have come together without the early support and encouragement of Leonard Stern, Laura Stern, and Jane Eickhoff. Jane also provided superb copy-editing skills for the price of a lunch, a wonderful bargain for me. The cover design and interior artwork was created by Mollye Hubbard: www.mollyehubbard.com

The many female friends who read early versions and told me how much they hated it also provided necessary motivation. I also have to thank Jane Zee for her knowledge and insight. It'd also be remiss if I didn't thank the dozens of women I've dated for helping me with the knowledge necessary to write this book.

Made in the USA
Lexington, KY
18 November 2011